11/88

To Ina—

Keep communicating!
Keep keep exploring!

— Marty

YOUR SEXUAL SECRETS

YOUR SEXUAL SECRETS

When to Keep Them, When and How to Tell

MARTY KLEIN

E. P. DUTTON NEW YORK

Published in the United States by E. P. Dutton,
a division of NAL Penguin Inc.,
2 Park Avenue, New York, N.Y. 10016.

Published simultaneously in Canada by
Fitzhenry and Whiteside, Limited, Toronto.

Library of Congress Cataloging-in-Publication Data

Klein, Marty.
     Your sexual secrets : when to keep them, when and how to tell /
Marty Klein.—1st ed.
       p. cm.
     ISBN 0-525-24716-5
     1. Sexual ethics. 2. Sex (Psychology) 3. Secrecy. 4. Intimacy
(Psychology) I. Title.
HQ32.K63   1988
306.7—dc19   88-11912
                                                               CIP

DESIGNED BY EARL TIDWELL

1 2 3 4 5 6 7 8 9 10
First Edition

To my parents, who taught me I could do anything, and to my wife, who makes it all possible.

CONTENTS

ACKNOWLEDGMENTS

I am delighted to have the chance to publicly thank some of the most important people in my life.

I have been blessed by the attention of author, educator, and philosopher Dr. Sol Gordon. His books, Institute, and political commitment have touched our world, and my work, in a profound way.

There are not nearly enough good role models in this world. I have been lucky enough to know educator and author Dr. Michael Carrera. If just a small bit of his class and genuineness have rubbed off on me, I am extremely fortunate.

I am grateful to Dr. Hal Zina Bennett, Dr. Jack Morin, Dr. Diane Morrissette, and Carol Wells, R.N., for their active involvement in the development of the manuscript. I am even more grateful to be able to call them my friends.

I thank my beloved Santa Barbara mentors, Rose Pierce

and Ted Berkman, for their total availability and support of my work.

Much of my effectiveness as a therapist and social scientist is based on the creativity of others, whom I am pleased to acknowledge: Lonnie Barbach, Mary Calderone, Dorothy Dinnerstein, Warren Farrell, Eleanor Hamilton, Helen Singer Kaplan, Sheldon Kopp, Kristin Luker, Alice Miller, C. Wright Mills, and Bernie Zilbergeld.

My colleagues in the American Society of Journalists & Authors, the Society for the Scientific Study of Sex, and the California Association of Marriage & Family Therapists continue to nurture and teach me.

My agent, Michael Larsen, and my editor, Leslie Wells, have provided invaluable assistance.

And my patients continue to amaze me, train me, and deepen my respect for the human race.

PREFACE

I invite you to read this book as if it were written for you personally.

It was.

This book addresses some of your strongest feelings: your concerns about your sexual adequacy, about the size and shape of your body, about your ability to please a partner. And the guilt about what you think, feel, and want sexually.

Although I wrote this book just for you, the language can't always reflect that. So as you read the case examples, mentally insert details more relevant for you. Make the people in the stories older, or gay, or whatever else makes sense to you.

And remember that "partners" refers to more than just sexual partners. It means *relationship* partners, which can include a close friend, child, or parent. The sexual secrets we keep from them can be as important as the ones we keep from lovers or spouses.

As you read the cases, keep in mind the context in which these people gain their insights. It often takes months of weekly psychotherapy to create a single breakthrough. Don't think from reading these brief highlights that you're seeing it all. That would be magic, and therapy is not magic.

SEXUAL SECRETS IN THE AGE OF AIDS

In a book of this kind it would be negligent to ignore the way sexual secrets can be a matter of life and death. At this time, our world is suffering through the terrible epidemic of AIDS. This disease is spread primarily by dirty needles, blood transfusions, the birth process, and intimate sexual contact.

Reasonable people agree that knowingly infecting someone else is a hideous, brutal act. When you fail to inform a potential lover that you have AIDS or have tested HIV positive, you imply that you are AIDS-free. Such misleading behavior should be considered a lie. It cannot possibly be forgiven.

More commonly, some people withhold information about their background that puts them in a higher-than-normal risk category. They typically do this because they fear the truth would chase away potential sex partners.

This too is selfish, cowardly, and immoral. It completely contradicts the life-affirming spirit of sexuality. Because AIDS, at this time, is always fatal, the right to make an informed decision about taking a risk is absolutely crucial. When you withhold information about yourself, you rob a potential partner of this right.

By the time the AIDS crisis is over, our way of thinking about sex will have changed forever. I'm looking forward to it.

PART I

ANATOMY OF A SEXUAL SECRET

Sexual secrets are more than lies told to avoid punishment. They are the inevitable result of the way American children learn about sex.

The most important thing we learn about sex is not some fact or technical word. Rather, it is the very meaning of sexuality itself. Most of us are trained to feel abnormal about our sexuality. We are taught to feel that our curiosity and our questions are bad. Naturally, we feel obliged to hide our sexual thoughts, feelings, and behavior.

This book will challenge the way you think about sex. Its goal is to help you *own* your sexuality as a wholesome entity. Once you accomplish that, you can then decide how to handle specific issues. For example, you can decide what to keep secret and what to share.

This book will help you look at such questions as: What is healthy sexuality? What is a healthy relationship? You'll also, in Part I, begin to look at *patterns* in your relationships.

These patterns are often invisible to those most affected by them. This book will help make them visible so you can understand and decide what to do about them.

People frequently complain or get depressed about their relationship frustrations. Rarely do they take control of their destiny and examine, discuss, and create change in the relationship rules that cause their frustrations.

To take a step toward better relationships and a more fulfilling sexuality, turn the page. And if at any time you find yourself feeling defensive, take a deep breath, and tune in to the support available on whatever page you happen to be reading.

1

WHAT ARE SEXUAL SECRETS?

Concealment doesn't simply complicate understanding—it encourages misunderstanding.
—**PROFESSOR DEAN BARNLUND**

We live in a world that encourages sexual secrets. These secrets don't protect us or make our lives better the way they are supposed to. On the contrary, these secrets only cripple our true sexual self, which is hidden, ignored, denied, and distorted.

As a result, girls punish themselves for erotic thoughts about father or big brother. Boys furtively hide evidence of wet dreams. Both sexes try desperately not to masturbate. Everyone feels guilty.

Is there an eight year old somewhere who has no sexual secrets from Mom or Dad? Is there a thirty-eight year old anywhere who keeps no sexual secrets from spouse, lover, or best friend?

The two questions are virtually one, for the foundations of adult behavior are laid in childhood. Sexual learning, in particular, starts at birth.

How do we come to develop secrets about sex? When does this happen, and why? What exactly are sexual secrets, anyway?

SEXUAL SECRETS

Sexual secrecy is much broader than simple lying. Most of the clients with whom I work have found this a useful definition: *Sexual secret-keeping takes place whenever you withhold information about your sexuality. It also takes place when you passively allow a significant person in your life to believe misinformation or incorrect assumptions about your sexuality, regardless of where the mistaken ideas come from.*

Many people also keep sexual secrets from themselves. One way they do this is through "selective amnesia" about traumatic events, such as incest. Just as the body loses consciousness when overwhelmed by physical pain, so the mind protects itself by repressing overwhelming emotional pain.

Less dramatically, "self-secrecy" occurs when our true feelings are so unacceptable to us that we unconsciously cover them with other feelings. Many men, for example, cannot admit to themselves that they fear women's powerful sexuality. One way they often express this fear is through constant criticism. Various men I work with have found fault with their wives' housekeeping, spending habits, sense of humor, and career commitment. Ironically, the secret-keeping magnifies the fear and intensifies the inner conflict.

Every relationship has unspoken expectations about communication, trust, and closeness that help define secrecy for the people involved. Say that you have had a vasectomy. Not mentioning this during a one-night stand is one thing. Not disclosing it to a fiancée is quite another. Allowing her to assume, by your silence, that you are fertile can create enormous problems.

Trust in relationships is vulnerable to both honest disagreement and not-so-honest manipulation. Everyone has a sexual history, sexual feelings, and sex-related beliefs. Do you and your partner agree on how much of these are relevant to your relationship?

If your definition of "relevant information" has ever differed with someone else's, you've probably been told (or said) things such as "How could you not tell me?" or "What do you mean you figured what I didn't know couldn't hurt me?" or "No, I don't understand that it just never came up."

Such comments reflect anger and humiliation. That's how people feel when they no longer know where they stand, or what their relationships' agreements are. It's like having your sense of reality challenged. You have no idea what's next.

What unstated expectations about communication do you and your partners have about:

- Subjects you are not supposed to raise with each other
- Aspects of the relationship you are not to discuss with anyone else
- How disagreements should be handled
- How affection should be expressed
- How you get each other's attention
- How criticism is best delivered
- How you each handle feeling misunderstood

KINDS OF SEXUAL SECRETS

In our culture, every conceivable aspect of sexuality is subject to secrecy. Common sexual secrets include faked orgasms, extra-marital relationships, fantasies about making love with a person of the same sex, and the experience of having been molested in childhood.

Last year, some of my students tried to think of a sex-related subject that no one hides. Take a moment right now and try this yourself.

Brainstorming in small groups, we found ourselves stymied. Finally, a likely candidate emerged: the enjoyment of sex itself. (As my uncle used to say: "Of all my relations, I like sex the best.") But even this simple acknowledgment is subject to secrecy.

Many of us are taught, for example, that women don't really enjoy sex. They either like the closeness, the tradition goes, or they use sex to acquire and manipulate husbands. I have counseled many women who feared they were "over-sexed" because they had a strong, healthy sex drive. And I have worked with many men who questioned the "morality" of wives or girlfriends who openly enjoy sexual pleasure.

As a result of such pressure, many women hide their interest in sex from friends, men in general, the man or woman they're involved with, and even themselves. So we can't really say that "I like sex" is never a sexual secret.

Some students suggested that the simple admission of having sex is never subject to secrecy. But we realized that many people hide that too, including teens, unmarried and widowed adults, priests, and senior citizens. Most nursing homes, in fact, report that the adult children of their residents expect the home to prevent sexual activity.

Several other possible nonsecrets were considered but rejected. They include "I'm a virgin" "I hate homosexuals" "I like my body" "I want to get pregnant" and "You turn me on." The class had to admit they couldn't think of a single aspect of sexuality that some people aren't hiding from themselves or others.

Certain themes did, however, emerge. Thus, the categories of sexual secrets we will use in this book are:

• Arousal and response
• Fears and fantasies

• The past
• Deliberate deception

WHY SECRECY?

There are many explanations for the common activity of sexual secret-keeping. But on close examination, some of the most obvious ones are inadequate. Let's look at these first.

Explanation 1: Secrecy is "natural."
American society distorts virtually every part of what might be our "natural" sexual expression. Gentleness in men, assertiveness in women, sensuous non-genital touching, the guilt-free enjoyment of masturbation, and the ability to celebrate monogamy must be considered unnatural in our culture, because they are severely inhibited.

And yet, other cultures around the world consider these expressions quite natural. So even if sexual secrecy were, in fact, "natural," that wouldn't make it any more likely to appear in our behavior.

Nor is our American form of sexual expression "natural" by the rest of the world's standards. Many tribal cultures are far more permissive than ours. In today's Scandinavian families, children and parents routinely acknowledge and discuss sexual behavior. They consider our secrecy and denial quite backward—and, by the way, have a teen pregnancy rate a small fraction of ours.

These societies contrast starkly with Inis Beag, an Irish island described by anthropologist John C. Messenger as the most erotically barren place on earth. Marriages there are arranged, and premarital sex is unknown. Adults do not bathe themselves between neck and knee. Considered indulgent, breast-feeding is rare. And sex is only for procreation: men feel debilitated by the loss of semen, while women endure sex as a distasteful duty.

These particular cultures have differing ideas about the

"naturalness" of secrecy. In fact, the dramatically different norms of these societies argue eloquently against using "naturalness" to explain any sexual behavior. "Natural" sexuality? No one in our modern age can ever, unfortunately, know what that is.

Explanation 2: Human sexuality is ugly, bad, or destructive, and should be hidden.

Our nineteenth-century ancestors were so obsessed with the destructive power of sex that they saw its dangers everywhere. They covered the legs of furniture, for example, for fear that men would be reminded of women's legs and get aroused. And they renamed the breasts and thighs of poultry so families wouldn't need to speak such words. Did you know that that's why we now refer to light meat and dark meat?

Laughable though this may seem, many people who oppose modern sex education share the same underlying attitude. They believe that if we don't tightly control the sexuality of adolescents, it will run wild and destroy us all. These fearful people have even arranged for their local high school libraries to ban books such as *The Diary of Anne Frank, The Color Purple,* and *Catcher in the Rye.* They are convinced, despite the examples of Nazi Germany and the Soviet Union, that secrecy can protect them.

The Bible is frequently invoked to justify sexual secrecy, but when it is, one wonders which Bible is used. Could it be the Bible that celebrates God's creation of our bodies? The Bible of Soloman's erotic Song of Songs? The Bible that talks of passionate love between husband and wife? Some people use the Bible the way others use astrology—to justify whatever beliefs and feelings they bring to it.

Fear of sexuality leads to the belief that sex is bad and secrecy is good. The fact, however, is that these beliefs are destructive and spiritually empty. Facing and letting go of sexual fear is a healthier, more life-affirming choice.

Explanation 3: Our partners can't handle our secrets.

Many people believe, correctly or not, that their partners are unable to handle sexual honesty. This makes sharing secrets seem like a poor idea, while secrecy looks like a good way of protecting one's partner. This explanation is usually accompanied by "good" reasons such as:

- "Anyone with my background is a slut, and no man wants a slut."
- "Her ego is too fragile."
- "It would remind him of his awful first marriage."
- "It would destroy her to know."
- "He'd kill my father."

But there's something suspicious here. Most people believe that *they* could handle the truth about their *partner's* sexuality. Yet we believe that our *partners* can't handle the very same truths about *us*.

Everyone can't be stuck with a partner less open than they are. In many cases, our beliefs about our partner's inflexibility are more about us than they are about our partners. These judgments tend to be tenacious, persisting in the face of contrary evidence.

Do you believe your mate just can't handle the truth? Have you checked it out with him or her lately? Would you know if you were wrong? Could you allow your mate to be more tolerant than you imagined? How would your life change if you found out your partner *could* handle your secret?

Can you take yes for an answer?

AN ALTERNATIVE EXPLANATION

Many people magnify their partners' shortcomings to rationalize their own unwillingness to be honest. But assume for a moment that people keep secrets to protect themselves. From what? From the negative consequences of sexuality that we're trained, as children, to expect.

Most American children are taught that their innocent sexuality is *bad*. You may have learned this lesson by growing up in a home where sex was never discussed, or spoken about only scornfully. Some people recall specific moments of learning that sexuality is dangerous: when they first had a sexual thought criticized as abnormal, for example, or when they were punished for masturbating.

Here are some of the ways we absorb negativity about sex as we grow up:

• We are caught and punished simply for expressing our sexuality. Perhaps you were caught masturbating, or found playing with a friend's genitals ("Playing doctor" is the way we used to do it) as a child.

• We are told directly by parents, teachers, and other adults that sex is bad. When my neighbor June was a child, for example, she was frequently warned by an aunt that "Boys only want one thing—to touch you under your clothes." Although June didn't understand quite why, she says, "My aunt's tone made it clear that this was a horrible thing."

A related message you may have been told is that any girl who enjoys that sort of thing is a "tramp." "I didn't know what that meant either," says June, "but it was obviously bad."

• We observe our parents' behavior toward each other. If there is no physical affection, if one parent always pushes the other's hand away, if one parent criticizes the other's sexual references or gestures, an observing child learns that sex is not a nice thing for people to share.

• We experience our parents' discomfort in relating to our genitals. They give them funny names (like "woo-woo," or worse, "down there"), refuse to touch or wash them, and discourage questions about them. This contrasts sharply with the parental approval we often get for the rest of our body.

• We notice the way sex education is handled. Most schools don't have any. Those that do frequently dump it on the teachers with the least seniority, who often receive no training in the subject.

Schools offering sex education typically require parental permission, even when the class is supposed to be mandatory. This, of course, is not true of math or history. The message that kids get from this is that information about sex is somehow dangerous.

Most parents and school officials are joined in an unholy alliance to deny children the information they need to make healthy sexual choices and lead healthy lives. Kids are smart enough to know this, but they aren't sophisticated enough to understand why. They come to the obvious conclusion that sex is bad. They learn to use this evil power to express anger against adults—to everyone's detriment.

• We participate in religions that are anti-sexual. Masturbation and sexual fantasy are considered sinful by most denominations. This means that virtually 100 percent of the children from these religious backgrounds are labeled bad, and feel guilty.

• We are bombarded with mass entertainment and advertising that is at bottom anti-sexual. The media exploit and distort sexual curiosity and interest; check any soap opera or beer ad. But at the same time, they fail to present sexuality as it really is. They could do this, for example, through contraceptive ads or the appropriate mention of birth control in programming.

When sexuality is seriously discussed in the media, it is generally presented as part of a problem, such as AIDS or teen pregnancy. Sexuality is rarely portrayed as something to celebrate, such as the way it enhances marriage, or the way touching humanizes medical environments.

In all, the lessons we learn about sex during childhood are consistently destructive.

THE SECRECY IMPERATIVE

In these different ways, sex is linked with shame, guilt, fear, and anxiety. Learning that sex in general is destructive, children apply that judgment to their own sexuality. Their simplistic moralism combines with their simplistic logic; they think, "Sex is bad. I am sexual. Therefore I am bad." Thus, sexuality is a focus of punishment and rejection, and the expression of personal inadequacy.

The experience of parental rejection over sexual issues has a profound impact. As children, we are keenly aware that our sheer survival depends on the care and good will of our parents. Thus, kids fear that disapproval will be followed by abandonment—and thus death. (This legacy is one reason that American adults are so phobic about rejection.)

Along with the young of every other species, human children are programmed for one thing: survival. And if kids believe that that requires hiding this problematic thing called sex, they will do so. This is the origin of what I call "The Secrecy Imperative": *The belief that to survive, you* must *hide your sexual thoughts, feelings, and behavior*. It's a sensible coping skill for surviving in an inexplicably hostile environment.

This belief may or may not be conscious. In adulthood, the survival it attempts to ensure is psychological, rather than physical—which is every bit as meaningful.

So years before puberty, young people develop sexual secrets. Freud believed that the time between roughly six and eleven years of age was a "latency period." To gain distance from their own incestuous and aggressive drives, he believed, children "sublimated" their sexual energy into schoolwork and chores.

Current research has refined that notion. Ronald and Juliette Goldman's enormous cross-cultural study shows that children *continue* developing their sexual interests, concepts, and vocabulary during this time. They simply do it as far from adult discovery as possible, having learned the rules of the adult world.

This leads to enormous internal conflict. We continue learning the adult values that promise survival, which contradict the wisdom we keep hearing from our bodies and hearts. For example, how many of the following stifling guidelines do you remember learning?

- "It's not ladylike to sit with your legs open."
- "Real men don't cry."
- "Remember, boys only want one thing from girls."
- "If a girl lets you touch her, she's not 'nice.' "
- "When they say 'no' they mean 'yes.' "
- "You'll have to do it, or he'll leave you for another girl."

The child's unsophisticated mind sees the world in simple black-and-white contrasts. We tend to overlearn the lessons of childhood. So not surprisingly, secrecy continues to evolve in adolescence. Increasingly self-aware, teenagers develop an additional pattern: secrecy from self.

Many young women, for example, refuse to carry condoms or a diaphragm on a date, unable to admit to themselves that they are considering having intercourse. Later that night, feeling passion's urgency or a sense of obligation, they acquiesce to unprotected sex. As educator Carol Cassell notes in *Swept Away,* they rationalize this as something that has happened *to* them, rather than something they have created.

The inventory of an individual's secrets continues to grow during sexual maturity. The Secrecy Imperative operates even as people create intimate, long-term relationships with both lovers and friends. There is a simple logic to what is hidden away: "If it's about my sexuality, it's probably not okay."

It doesn't even matter how reasonable or enjoyable the behavior is. The capacity for multiple orgasms, for example, can be deeply satisfying. But it may also contradict a self-image of demure, controlled, ladylike, and never more passionate than my partner. I have seen many women who felt it was necessary to hide this exciting part of their sexuality, or even lose it.

This is the result of a profound sense of being *bad*. Since we cannot accept ourselves, we cannot imagine being accepted by someone else. That is why most people say, "Yes, I could probably handle my partner's sexual secrets, but I don't think my partner could handle mine."

Most of us believe, unconsciously, that we *must* keep sexual secrets, still attempting to survive as we did when children. We are like the confused old Japanese soldiers on those Pacific islands still fighting World War II today.

The Secrecy Imperative, then, is why sexual secrecy is so ubiquitous. Psychological survival depends on it in childhood, and we never lose the commitment to it as we mature. As adults living in a profoundly anti-sexual world, why should we?

In the next chapter we'll look at how sexual secrets affect you and your relationships. This will help you make informed choices, which you will have a chance to do in Part III.

2

EFFECTS OF
SEXUAL
SECRETS

*He felt separate, alone, not able to reach out to anyone. So
he bought a book called How to Hug—and discovered, when
he got home, that it was volume nine of the encyclopedia.*
—MORT SAHL

Now that you know what a sexual secret is and how we learn
to keep them, let's look at how sexual secrets affect us. This
chapter examines four problems associated with sexual secret-
keeping:

- How secrets can isolate us from those we love
- How secrets can lower our self-esteem
- How secrets can contribute to sexual problems
- How secrets prevent the healing of emotional wounds

We will explore each of these through the words and experiences of people who have struggled with them.

ISOLATION

As we have seen, keeping sexual secrets from your mate is an understandable, very human thing to do. It's sometimes so automatic that you're not even aware of doing it. This doesn't mean, however, that it is a harmless activity.

Keeping sexual secrets leads to isolation from our mates. The secrets prevent us from being known for who we really are. And the more we hold back, the more we become isolated from ourselves, as our fear of discovery inhibits self-expression, especially during sex.

Secrecy also leads to isolation because it prevents the healing of traumatic sexual experiences from the past. This is significant because about one in five American families is touched by some form of sexual abuse or sexual violence. Most of these crimes remain hidden, because most victims never tell a single person.

Ultimately, secrecy makes sex a dangerous activity, because this is the likeliest place your secret will be discovered. Ordinarily, the pleasure and closeness of sex invite you to relax and let go each time you make love. But if you're keeping secrets, you must fear the way that every form of sexual expression—such as low desire or unusual turn-ons—might give you away.

When you keep secrets, even your sexual partner becomes an enemy. The person closest to you becomes the most threatening, always on the verge of stumbling onto your secret. Emotional withdrawal is the only "sensible" solution. Feelings of isolation and alienation are inevitable.

This is exactly what happened with one teacher caught in the isolation trap. Gail, a tall woman who fidgeted with her curly hair, came into therapy feeling frustrated and pessimistic.

"Sex just isn't satisfying for me," she said, "and there doesn't seem to be anything I can do about it. I want sex less and less, which I think is unfair to Sam. But with his narrow attitudes, I just can't be me. If he were different, I could ask for oral stimulation, and enjoy sex a lot more. But I'm afraid that he just wouldn't accept it if I told him. So I don't say anything."

Gail paused, then continued. "Some days it's easy. But some days I get furious, although I try not to let on. It's especially hard when sex is blah and Sam asks what's the matter. I say nothing, and then I feel a million miles away from him.

"Can you help me enjoy sex more?" she asked. "I feel terribly alone."

As we talked, it became clear that Gail was uncomfortable with any kind of conflict. One of her roles in the marriage, in fact, was steering the two of them away from arguments.

"Especially about sex," she sadly agreed when I raised the point. "Since it's my demands that the fights would be about, it's up to me to keep things calm. I do that by keeping quiet at certain times about what I want."

Occasionally, we'd have a session when Gail didn't feel self-critical. She would then feel righteous about her "sacrifice," and how her-lack of openness helped keep "harmony" in the marriage. But although she meant well, her strategy wasn't working. Her secret-keeping and emotional withdrawal weren't solving the problem—they were part of the problem.

After about two months of therapy, Gail started to let herself feel the anger that had been accumulating for years. I then suggested that she and Sam come in together. Their first joint session started out friendly, but then Sam made a joke about Gail not being all there during sex. That was when she finally exploded.

"I'm not all there because I'm not getting what I want," Gail shouted. "If you were always hiding, you'd have trouble being warm and loving too." The truth was out. Gail paused, then shrugged and told the whole story. Sam was astounded. He hadn't realized Gail was sacrificing in the way she described. He certainly had not asked her to.

Sam admitted to Gail that he preferred her to climax from intercourse instead of oral sex. "It makes me feel more manly," he said. "But I never realized this whole thing was such a big deal for you. I just want to feel close to you when we have sex together."

The following diagram shows how the isolation resulting from secrecy reinforces itself over time:

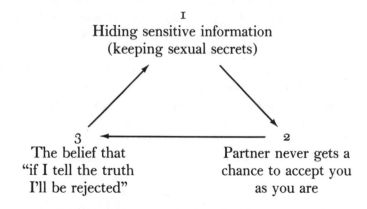

I
Hiding sensitive information
(keeping sexual secrets)

3
The belief that
"if I tell the truth
I'll be rejected"

2
Partner never gets a
chance to accept you
as you are

1. Withholding sensitive information . . .
2. Prevents your partner from demonstrating his/her love and acceptance, and this . . .
3. Perpetuates the belief that telling the truth will lead to rejection, which leads to . . .
1. Withholding sensitive information.

Within this classic vicious circle, isolation takes on a life of its own instead of eventually fading away. That's why choosing to keep a secret is serious business: it separates you from the person you want to feel close to, and keeps you from getting back.

LOWERED SELF-ESTEEM

Low self-esteem is a second, related effect of keeping sexual secrets. You've heard of the new book for people with poor self-image? It's called *Looking Out for Number 3 or 4.*

Imagine finding out that your best friend's mate has never said "I know you and love you exactly the way you are." You'd be sad for both of them, wouldn't you? Yet this is what secret-keeping guarantees: a mate who doesn't know who you really are, who therefore has no chance to *accept* the way you really are.

In most relationships, self-revelation tends to be done on roughly the same level by both parties. When you hesitate to reveal information about yourself, you invite your partner to hesitate as well. If you keep secrets, therefore, you are far less likely to learn how much your sexuality has in common with that of other people, particularly in the areas you keep secret. In short, secret keeping makes it harder to know that you're "normal."

Finally, the guilt people usually feel about keeping sexual secrets also lowers self-esteem. Withholding information from someone we care about breaks an unspoken rule that most relationships have ("We won't keep anything important from each other"). In addition, the hiding and secretiveness recall our childhood experiences of sneaking around and breaking rules. Everyone who keeps secrets feels, at times, like a "bad child."

Take another look at how the isolation of secrecy perpetuates itself. You can see how lowered self-esteem fits right into our model:

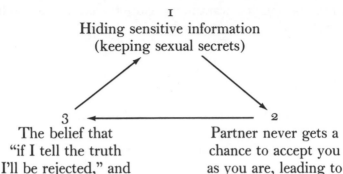

I
Hiding sensitive information
(keeping sexual secrets)

3
The belief that
"if I tell the truth
I'll be rejected," and
lowered self-esteem

2
Partner never gets a
chance to accept you
as you are, leading to
lowered self-esteem

1. Withholding sensitive information . . .
2. Prevents your partner from demonstrating his/her love and acceptance. This lowers self-esteem and . . .
3. Perpetuates the belief that telling the truth will lead to rejection, which lowers self-esteem and leads to . . .
1. Withholding sensitive information.

You probably know that risk-taking is a crucial part of truly intimate relationships. Unfortunately, both isolation and low self-esteem make risk-taking difficult. If you keep secrets, you fear rejection. Performance for its sake becomes more important than sharing the pleasures of closeness. Real communication is compromised. The delightful process of sharing new parts of yourself is discouraged, which threatens a relationship with going stale.

In Gail's case (and perhaps you can see the same pattern in yours), isolation and low self-esteem led to uncomfortable feelings such as anger, frustration, and disappointment. It's common to feel betrayed by a partner who you imagine is judging you. In fact, when we expect people to judge us we subtly encourage them to do so. Our suspicions are then justified.

Since such feelings jeopardize our ability to keep secrets,

we can only express them indirectly. Ways of acting them out include bullying people; using money-making or other ways to prove our self-worth; and behaving self-destructively, through alcohol abuse, dangerous hobbies, and so on. Constant criticism was the way I did it in my very first relationship.

These feelings and behaviors actively detract from high self-esteem. But relationships work best with partners who feel good about themselves. That's one reason secrecy makes intimacy difficult.

SEXUAL PROBLEMS

Nobody has ever walked into my office and said, "I keep sexual secrets and it's hurting my relationship."

But I have noticed that secrets are a predictable factor in a wide range of sexual problems. Hiding who we are, what we want, how we feel, or what happened in the past prevents us from creating the relaxation, trust, and enthusiasm that satisfying sex requires.

If you are sexually dissatisfied, ask yourself if you're keeping one or more sexual secrets. If you are, sex may be uncomfortable, because:

- It threatens to seduce you into letting down your guard, perhaps betraying your secrets
- It's the activity where your partner typically invites closeness, spontaneity, and enthusiasm
- Its very intimacy makes you more vulnerable to your own self-criticism.

Contrary to what most people believe, creating great sex requires very little *doing*. Rather, it involves relaxing, opening the senses, and accepting yourself and your partner.

Sexual secrets, on the other hand, compel you to hide your body, worry about your performance, fear that your partner is getting bored, or hope that you won't be discovered or rejected. By the time you've done all that, sex is over and you've missed the experience.

Sexual difficulties come in many forms. There are dysfunctions, such as erection and orgasm problems; there is impaired and exaggerated desire; there are medical problems; and there is lack of enjoyment. Each can be created, maintained, or worsened by sexual secrets. Following are several examples.

The first is Ann, a twenty-nine-year-old dancer who was quite self-confident on a public stage, but very self-conscious in private with her boyfriend.

COMPLAINT: Lack of orgasm with partner
SECRET: Preferences, turn-ons, and response
FEAR: Being judged; turning off partner

"When I'm alone I have great orgasms," Ann told me. "I know just what to do, and I take plenty of time. But I would never tell my boyfriend I masturbate. Jeff would think he wasn't satisfying me. He's already frustrated that I usually don't climax with him."

Since Ann was verbally shy, I suggested she might use her hands or body to communicate with Jeff.

"Show him what to do?" she asked. She rolled her green eyes. "No, I'd be too embarrassed. Besides, if he saw the kind of touching I like, he'd probably think I was weird. Believe me, when I do it alone at home I'm not very ladylike!

"I wish he would just figure out what to do." She paused. "Well, part of me does. Part of me doesn't, because when I come I really moan and sweat and stuff, and I don't know how he'd react to that." Quietly, Ann added, "I hope you're not going to force me to talk to him about this . . . I really don't want to risk losing him."

Ann knew how to have orgasms. But she didn't feel comfortable sharing the information with her boyfriend. As a result, sex had become a problem that was maintaining distance between them. You can imagine Ann quietly getting angrier and angrier. Over time, her anger, sexual frustration, and pessimism could easily lower her sex drive.

Like most people, Ann hadn't made an explicit decision to hide information about herself; rather, she felt she *had to*. This obligation was based on a fantasy of her boyfriend's reaction, a fantasy that was much more about her than it was about him. She was hoping her secrecy would prevent Jeff from judging and leaving her. Ironically, her secrecy was exactly what was pushing them apart.

When she began working with me, Ann couldn't consider the possibility of Jeff accepting her true sexuality. At some point in the relationship, she had simply settled for dissatisfaction. But after twelve sometimes-stormy weeks of therapy, Ann no longer felt like a bad person. She decided to share her secret with Jeff.

The result? "He was delighted," said a smiling Ann. "He said he'd be willing to try what I liked. And get this—he said he couldn't understand what I had been so afraid about, and why I was so surprised at his reaction!"

Like most people, Jeff was far more open to Ann's secret than she feared he'd be. Her inaccurate assumptions resulted from projecting her negative self-judgment ("My sexuality is bad") onto him ("He thinks my sexuality is bad"). This is how her secrecy helped maintain a painful, unnecessary sexual problem.

Another example of sexual secrecy concerns an event from the past. I thought this might be so when Jane, an attractive mother of three, started our first session highly concerned about confidentiality.

COMPLAINT: Low desire
SECRET: Previous pregnancy
FEAR: Unwanted pregnancy; being judged a "tramp"

"I don't understand why my sex drive is so low," said Jane during that first session. She loved her husband, a "good-looking, warm, considerate man." Telling me about her sexual history, Jane hesitated frequently, nervously covering her face with her hand periodically. I had the feeling she was concealing something. When subtle encouragement failed to uncover it, I shared my suspicion with Jane. Looking at me, she sighed and plunged ahead.

"I never told my husband about the pregnancy and abortion," she said. "It happened before I met him, and I didn't think it mattered." I looked at her encouragingly and said nothing. "Okay, it would be more honest to say I was afraid of his reaction."

She shrugged. "At first, I didn't want him to think I'd been, y'know, a tramp when I was younger. Eventually, it just became impossible to tell him. For one thing, it never came up; I mean, you don't just casually announce, 'Oh, by the way, six years ago I was pregnant and had an abortion.' "

Contrary to the popular concept of "frigidity," low desire frequently develops in sexually active people for whom sex becomes dangerous or painful. Jane *wanted* to desire sex more, but fear about being discovered and judged prevented her from thinking about sex as joyful.

I also suspected another fear. Did she, like many people who have had unintentional pregnancies, fear another?

"Yes," Jane said. "I try not to think about it, but every once in a while I catch myself in the middle of sex thinking, 'What if it happens again?' "

So here was another way in which sex felt dangerous. And because of her commitment to secrecy, Jane couldn't really enlist Tom's help in sharing the emotional load.

I told Jane that as long as lovemaking reminded her of the secret she couldn't reveal, she wouldn't be free to relax and express herself sexually.

"I guess I understand that," she said reluctantly. "And I

know Tom will get fed up with this 'not tonight' routine sooner or later."

I agreed. "Eventually, you'll have to do something about this," I said, "even if it only involves reinterpreting your secret as an acceptable part of the past."

Jane's response was grim. "I prefer not to think about the future right now," she said quietly. Jane saw me for about eight sessions. At that point, she decided not to share her secret with Tom. Not surprisingly, her interest in sex had by then disappeared altogether. Some people's stories don't have happy endings.

The next instance also involves low sexual desire, but in this case, Randy was keeping a secret from himself. It was understandable; knowing his true feelings really was threatening his relationship. Randy's ignorance was costly, however. It was costing him his sex drive.

COMPLAINT: Low desire
SECRET: Does not want a baby
FEAR: Domestic conflict

Randy was the kind of guy people like as soon as they meet, and I did too. An attractive man, he was well-dressed in a casual, understated way. We made a bit of small talk, and then his smiling face darkened.

"I'm really confused about losing interest in sex. Cathy and I used to make love all the time when we were dating, and I enjoyed it a lot. We even got off on the same things, like oral sex. Even now, we only have one small disagreement. She wants a baby more than I do."

That's an interesting clue, I remember thinking. I asked for some details about it. "Actually," said Randy, "she wants a baby right now, and I don't. In three or four years, maybe, but not now, not when we're both so busy with our careers and having so much fun traveling."

I asked if they had had many arguments about the baby issue. "Oh yeah, lots," Randy said, shaking his head. "It used to get pretty bad—Cathy getting depressed, talking about how she's already getting old and that soon it would be too late. I just can't handle her disappointment and crying. So we don't talk about it much anymore."

"But not talking about an issue doesn't mean it has gone away," I said.

Randy agreed. "The question is still unresolved, I know," he replied. "It's like a cloud over our lovemaking. Almost every time we do it she looks at me as if to say, 'This is another time that I could be getting pregnant.'"

"You sound angry," I observed.

"Oh, a little," said Randy, trying to sound casual. "I get mad sometimes—why does she have to ruin sex for us like that? But I also feel guilty for not giving her what she wants so much."

I asked Randy to look at his hands. To his surprise, he saw that his fists were tightly clenched. Maybe he was angrier than he realized, I suggested. He denied it, but looked thoughtful.

"Sometimes I even worry that she'll forget to take her birth control pills," he continued. "One way or another, I guess this thing is on my mind more than I'd like." He paused. "But what has this all got to do with not wanting to have sex?"

I knew it wouldn't work to confront Randy with a truth that he was working so hard to avoid. So, for several weeks we went slowly. One day "the kid thing," as he called it, came up again.

"Why can't she just wait a year or two?" he asked.

"You know," I replied, "I can imagine you saying that same thing every year for the next ten years."

"If today's mood were permanent, that would be true," he agreed.

"Isn't it?" I inquired.

"It would be, if not for Cathy making me feel bad," he answered. I looked at him, and watched his face suddenly change.

"Do you think," he slowly asked, "that I don't want kids *at all?*" I was silent. "Have I been lying to her?" Randy asked.

"Maybe not so much to her," I gently suggested, "as to yourself."

The realization that Randy didn't want kids at all, of course, didn't resolve the marital problems right away. In fact, things became rougher for a while. But just acknowledging the truth made Randy feel much better—"as if I can breathe again," as he put it—and his sex drive began to return. Then he and Cathy were able to start talking about their future in a more productive, adult way.

Randy's story illustrates an important principle: when the consequences of sexual honesty are frightening, sex often loses its appeal. Frequently, other forms of intimacy become more difficult as well. Many secret-keepers are afraid of losing a relationship all at once. Instead, they lose it over time, piece by piece.

Joseph's story shows how secrecy can result in the need to control sexual interactions tightly. This dynamic made good sex extremely difficult for this security guard.

COMPLAINT: Frequent lack of erection
SECRET: Intense, "abnormal" fantasies
FEAR: Losing control; offending partner

"One of my favorite things during sex," Joseph told me in his second session, "is to imagine I'm with someone else. Sometimes I fantasize that I'm forcing someone to have sex, or that there's another girl there with us. Or that someone is watching us through the window, or listening to us."

Joseph paused, looking at me. I think he wanted to see if I was disgusted or shocked. Clearly, I was neither. I wasn't sure if he was pleased or disappointed.

"Basically, I have a lot of thoughts during sex that are, well, not quite normal, you see? Being impotent on top of that really makes sex a problem," he said. "See, mentally I'm going one hundred miles an hour, and in bed I'm just zero."

"I don't imagine that you've shared these fantasies with your partners," I said. "Of course not," he replied. But how about sharing his concerns *about* his thoughts, rather than the thoughts themselves—could he do that? "No, I wouldn't dare tell my lady friends about this," he said. "They'd run in the opposite direction, don't you think?"

Joseph was so scared of his own sexuality that he unconsciously prevented his erection. Sex had to be a carefully controlled activity, lest someone discover the "real" Joseph, who was naughtily sexual. Under such circumstances, it would feel dangerous to function normally.

Joseph needed to know just how common his fantasies were. During our time together, we discussed the possible value of joining a men's group, talking to friends, or reading popular self-help books like Bernie Zilbergeld's *Male Sexuality,* Shere Hite's *Report on Male Sexuality,* or Levine and Barbach's *The Intimate Male.*

My goal was to help Joseph realize that he is "normal." At that point, he could then *decide* whether or not he wanted to discuss his fantasies and experiences with a partner. Regardless of his choices, the perspective of "normalcy" would help Joseph regain a sense of calmness and safety about sex. That would be a crucial step toward having dependable erections. The jackpot would be for Joseph to decide to add a new dimension to what he wants in a woman: "someone I feel comfortable talking to."

When our work ended, that was exactly how Joseph described the "ideal mate" he was now looking for. I believe he'll find her, too.

This case is about masturbation. It's particularly poignant to me because I hear it so frequently—and because it involves such needless suffering.

COMPLAINT: Rapid ejaculation
SECRET: Masturbation
FEAR: Making partner feel inadequate; being judged "immature"

Ted was a veteran firefighter with large, calloused hands and a thick black mustache. His best friend had been in marriage counseling with me the previous year, "So you come highly recommended," he said. "But I have to tell you, I'm skeptical about shrinks. I want to be honest about that from the beginning.

"Anyway, the story is, I masturbated as a kid. We all did, right?" he began. "Well, one of my buddies got caught one time, and his grandmother almost killed him."

I've heard this story hundreds of times from both men and women. I don't know why, but on this particular day it reminded me of Truman Capote's line: "The one great advantage of masturbation is that you don't have to dress up for it."

Ted's voice snapped me back to his story. "Bobby's grandma told him he'd get terrible pimples, and that his penis would fall off. Bobby told me what happened, and we laughed about it for months afterwards. But when our faces broke out a year later we were petrified! We both tried to swear off, but it didn't work. How do you stop doing something that feels so good?

"Well, now I'm married," he continued. "I love my wife and the sex is fine, but once or twice a week I like to sneak off alone and give myself a good orgasm. But it's just like when I was a kid—in the bathroom, pretending to be doing something else. And definitely not taking my time. I do it as quickly as I can."

Ted's explanation of why he felt obliged to keep his secret was not unusual. "I know if my wife found out, she'd feel real bad, feel she wasn't satisfying me. It would almost be like I was being unfaithful. So I don't say anything."

Ted was suffering under a double burden. Unintentionally, he had trained himself to climax quickly. His hurried style of masturbation had been transferred to his lovemaking. In addition, his guilt was preventing him from relaxing and enjoying intercourse. This anxiety was also triggering the rapid ejaculation.

Ted's secrecy, of course, prevented his wife from accepting his interest, from reducing his guilt, and from giving him a chance to retrain himself to make love in a more relaxed way. Anxiety was an inevitable product of the secrecy—not of the masturbation, but of the secrecy around it.

Still not done with his early scares about masturbation, Ted was, metaphorically, stuck in childhood. He was still dealing with the profound experiential message that his sexuality is bad. Reversing this heritage and accepting his normalcy would be the first step toward improving Ted's functioning.

Incidentally, Ted could do this with or without his wife's support. Sharing the secret with her is not nearly as important as accepting it himself.

OLD EMOTIONAL WOUNDS

Millions of people have been traumatized through incest, child molestation, rape, or coerced sex while dating. In the past, our lack of understanding has led us to underestimate the frequency and impact of such events. In many cases we have even blamed the victim. You can understand why most people have felt obliged to keep such events secret.

These traumatic experiences almost always involve secrecy. The wrongdoer says "Don't tell your mother," or "Don't tell the police," or "If you tell my friends I'll deny it." Most victims maintain that secrecy later as adults. This is a terrible, painful repetition of the original victimization. This time, ironically, it is perpetrated by the victim him- or herself.

If trust and intimacy are to flourish in a relationship, sexually traumatic experiences must somehow be resolved. This is difficult under the best of circumstances. Self-imposed secrecy makes it even harder.

Secrecy prevents us from sharing the healing energy of our loved ones. Although some partners deal with their own pain by either blaming the victim or not believing the story, chances are strong that your partner will be supportive. Continued secrecy robs you of the chance to be accepted as you really are. It helps maintain your belief that there is something wrong with *you* because you were traumatized.

The belief that secrecy is mandatory keeps people living in the past—acting like victims who are still being coerced. Speaking out and seizing the *choice* of how to run your life—including whether, and whom to tell—ends the victim role for good.

That's the point of this story about Theresa, a woman whose body refused to have sex. She was almost in tears when she came to me about the problem. "We have a good marriage except for one thing," said the young homemaker. "Whenever we try to have intercourse, my vagina just clamps shut.

"At first, Roberto was patient," she sniffled, "but eventually we both became irritable and fought about it a lot. Doctors mostly gave me simple advice that didn't work, like have a glass of wine at bedtime to relax."

Eventually, one physician sent her to me for sex therapy. He had examined her and found no physical pathology. Suspecting that Theresa's problem was caused by a very bad sexual experience in the past, I gently suggested that such a past connection was not uncommon. She quickly changed the subject, which I allowed without comment.

Then, near the end of the session, she brought it up herself. "I never told anyone about it, because I was so ashamed," she said. "I certainly couldn't tell Roberto—I was afraid he'd kill my father. I just figured I had to live with it." The truth was out: as a young girl, Theresa had been molested by her father.

I asked Theresa to return later in the week. When she did, we discussed her family background and the abuse. I suggested she join a group for women who had been molested as children. She agreed to come in again after her first group meeting.

The following week, she told me all about the meeting, amazed at how many other women had stories just like hers. Feeling encouraged, she continued seeing me and attending the group. "Those people have made me feel normal and accepted for the first time in years," she said at one point.

About a month later, she said that several of the women were encouraging her to tell Roberto. "They say I won't feel so alone, that it will bring us closer. What do you think?" she asked.

We discussed it for several weeks. Finally, she made her decision. "I know you believe my sex problem is connected to the thing with my father. If that's true," she said steadily, "I don't think my marriage can afford my not talking about it anymore."

Theresa was scared, but she worked up the courage to tell her husband. The next week she came in ready to burst. "It was just like I was afraid it would be," she cried. "He yelled a lot, said crazy things. He wanted to run right out and kill my father," she sobbed.

At that point I asked to see Theresa and Roberto together. Although they clearly loved each other, the session was filled with accusations and tears. For weeks there were late-night phone calls between us. But eventually the power of their love triumphed. Roberto began to accept what had happened in the past, which allowed Theresa to finish accepting it herself.

"I've decided not to confront my father about this," Theresa told me one week. "I feel done." By the end of the session, I agreed with her. That's when we started a series of exercises to do at home. Sex became gradually easier, and within nine weeks she and Roberto were having enjoyable intercourse together.

Theresa's case is a vivid example of how secrecy can keep people imprisoned in the past. Finally speaking honestly about her trauma enabled Theresa to separate the dangerous past from the safe present. Her vaginal spasms went away soon after; they were no longer needed as protection from unwanted invasion.

LOOKING AHEAD

Can secrecy actually intensify sexual experience? Some sexologists believe that the strongest passions are flamed by rulebreaking. Secrecy, they argue, can help accomplish this when people break social taboos or relationship agreements. We'll examine this theory in the next chapter, which also explores other psychological "benefits" of secrecy. Sexual secrets can be an indirect expression of anger, provide a sense of power, and create a personal treasure all your own.

3

THE VALUE OF SEXUAL SECRETS

It may be called the Master Passion, the hunger for self-approval.

—MARK TWAIN

When I ask people why they keep sexual secrets, the most common answers they give are the fear of being rejected or punished and the fear of harming an important relationship.

These are the *conscious* reasons that people keep sexual secrets. On the unconscious level, people use secrecy to feel safe from their earliest childhood fears about closeness. In this chapter we will look at how these fears make secret-keeping feel important and valuable. The goal is to make you more conscious of your unconscious processes.

Sexual secrecy in relationships is a trade-off. By helping you feel less vulnerable to judgment and rejection, it can reduce the emotional turmoil you feel about intimacy, allowing you to enter and maintain relationships. But as we saw in

Chapter 2, secrecy also limits the depth and satisfaction of relationships. This is the price for that all-too-fleeting peace of mind.

It's not that we fool ourselves about our "real" reasons for secrecy. Just as it is for many victims of serious accidents, it is sometimes important for us to repress and therefore forget painful experiences. That's part of our human legacy. To protect us from a too intense moment, our mind sometimes files information about it in our unconscious.

So don't criticize yourself about your unconscious processes, or read these pages as criticism. This chapter—this book—is designed to help you understand, and therefore sympathize with, yourself.

WHY WE FEAR RELATIONSHIPS

We all, on some level, have fear about relationships. We learn about relationships as infants, when our needs are simple: to be kept warm, dry, and fed. When these needs are gratified, we experience relating as good. At other times, when our needs are frustrated, we learn that relating—that is, depending on others—is a mistake.

As long as our basic needs are reasonably satisfied, we can handle the frustrations. As psychologist D. W. Winnicott said, parents do not have to be perfect caregivers; they merely have to be "good enough." Interacting with "good enough" parents gives us, as infants, a positive attitude about closeness. We trust that our relationships will generally be satisfying, and that the inevitable bumps will be relatively short-lived.

Unfortunately, the characteristic innocence of the human infant's mind, coupled with the inexperience of most parents, seems to conspire against developing this general sense of safety. The still-incomplete infant brain cannot adequately cope with the everyday irritability, insecurity, or disappointments expressed by parents in the normal routine of living. Infants are not sophisticated enough to imagine that their own frustration may be the result of a parent's non-responsiveness, rather than their own inadequacies.

Here lies the terrible conflict of infancy: to be self-centered and demanding at the same time that we are 100 percent dependent on others' good will. The dependency is literal, for if the caregivers withdraw too much of their attention the infant will, in fact, die.

In this sense, infants experience situations in only one of two ways. A given moment either contributes to gratification, or it threatens total destruction. This need for immediate satisfaction is as complex as the undeveloped infant mind gets. If you've ever tried to encourage an infant to stop crying while you fix a bottle, you've experienced this first-hand.

Infants experience the threat of their own destruction in three forms: 1) "I'll be annihilated" 2) "I'll be suffocated," and 3) "I'll be abandoned." We carry this heritage with us all our lives. More than simply damaging our later relationships, it characterizes and partly determines them.

Thus, we enter adult relationships unconsciously afraid of being destroyed. Not just afraid of being rejected or hurt, but afraid of being *destroyed*.

HOW SECRECY PRODUCES THE ILLUSION OF SAFETY

In spite of our fears, we still have the need to relate. The human animal needs others to speak with and bond with, to touch and to nurture. Without these, we grow physically and emotionally ill.

The human dilemma, therefore, is this: How can I fulfill my need to relate while also protecting myself from the perceived threat of annihilation? And how can I do this without somehow pushing away those close to me, destroying the magic relationships I need to survive?

Most people solve this existential problem by constructing their intimate relationships in a special way. They choose a format that allows them to feel *somewhat* close when they most want to, while allowing them to deny or destroy the closeness when that feels necessary.

Such a relationship would have to be created in a particular way. You'd have to avoid being real enough that someone else could truly know you, pin you down, and possibly destroy you. You'd have to develop and relate through a pseudo-self—a contrived image of a person rather than a whole, real person.

Sexual secrecy is one way to accomplish this. It allows you to manipulate who your partner thinks you are. It's easy to justify doing this, because of the unspoken cultural agreement that people can't handle each other's sexual feelings, thoughts, and behavior.

Keep in mind that this strategy only makes you *feel* safer. You don't get the intimacy of real acceptance. You only get the pseudo-intimacy of feeling safe from attack.

SPECIFICS

There are four ways in which sexual secrecy lets us feel safer and less frightened of being destroyed while relating. These ways allow us to:

1. Seize power
2. Create distance
3. Act out feelings
4. Fulfill the demands of unconscious childhood scripts

Use these overlapping categories to examine how *you* value secrecy. Each is discussed below.

Seizing power

As a secret-keeper, you can seize power by influencing various aspects of closeness, such as the level of trust, nurturance, sexual satisfaction, and cooperation.

Secrecy can also be a way of controlling information. You can decide what your partner will know about you and your relationship. Through secrecy you can give yourself a different past, and therefore control the direction of the present.

Another way in which secrecy can be used to seize power is in the creation and maintenance of a personal treasure—some fact, experience, feeling, or object that only you control. The treasure can be so personal that no one else knows it even exists. Examples could be a sexual encounter with someone famous, a tattoo on your inner thigh, and your preference for cross-dressing when out of town on business.

Finally, secrecy can make relationships seem safer by the power they give you to prevent sexual bonding, which may feel dangerous or dirty.

The story of a software designer I once worked with illustrates this well. Although she had great difficulty reaching orgasm with her boyfriend Dan, Tammy refused to tell him the kind of touching that aroused her most. "He should know by now," she insisted. "Besides, it's so unromantic— 'A little to the left. Now harder. Now slower.' The whole idea turns me off."

Tammy was very frustrated about what she called the "incompleteness" of the sex she had with Dan. Yet, she only did the homework I assigned about half the time. She sometimes came to our sessions late, and even left early for a dinner appointment once. When I questioned her about such behavior, she shrugged it off.

Obviously, some part of Tammy did not want the sexual problem fixed, but it wouldn't have been helpful to come right out and say that. So I asked her to close her eyes and imagine a scene from her future, after the successful completion of therapy.

"Imagine that it is six months from now, Tammy, and your orgasm problem is solved." I paused to let her get into the fantasy. "But you seem unhappy," I suggested. "Your shoulders are slumped, your face is frowning, and your legs are tightly crossed. Clearly, having orgasms easily has created other problems. What's wrong?"

"Dan knows all my tricks now," said Tammy, speaking from her imagined future. "He's used to me climaxing every time. And he wants sex a lot." I asked Tammy what that was like. "He's taking it for granted," she said. "Sex is taking over. He thinks whenever he wants to love me we can just go to bed and have a good time."

We were finally getting to the bottom of things. "And what's the matter with that?" I asked.

"It's not right," she replied, "the two of us just making love, as if there were nothing wrong with it. But there is. Sex can take over, turn you into a slave."

Tammy's unconscious had spoken: her fantasy of life without sexual secrecy was full of pressure and danger. So Tammy had a good reason to prevent sex from becoming too enjoyable. She was using her sexual secret to "survive" the dangers of sexuality.

Of course, the reality was that she was in no danger of becoming a "sex slave." But Tammy's unconscious—like everyone else's—had a "reality" all its own. The task of therapy was to defuse the unnecessary fear it produced.

That's just what happened. Once Tammy was less afraid of bonding sexually with Dan, she was much more willing to share her secret—her "tricks," as she called them.

Sexual secrecy sometimes does create the illusion of power in relationships. We'll discuss the incomplete and sometimes destructive nature of this power later on.

Creating distance

Secrecy is also a way to create distance. For people who fear closeness, the ability to do this feels critically important. You might, unconsciously, want to create distance when your partner is offering support, such as empathy, affection, or practical help. For example, refusing to tell a current partner that you had been raped by a previous one—and that you had fears about being victimized again—would create distance and reduce any unconscious concern about being too dependent.

One way people create distance through sexual secrecy is by adopting the role of martyr. One man I worked with used to complain quite loudly about "having" to give his wife oral sex.

"Martha doesn't know how much I dislike the smell of her vagina," Harold told me. "But since she enjoys me eating her so much, I do it. The whole thing feels yucky, though. God, being married is no picnic."

Harold never discussed this with Martha, and his frustration grew. It was surely a painful situation for him. At the same time, though, his martyr role fit like a comfortable shoe. It provided a "reason" for him not to be close to Martha, and for their sex together to be adversarial rather than shared.

Secret longing for a past lover or relationship can also create distance. It can make a present partner or relationship look gray and uninviting, reducing your interest in sexual contact. That can chill a relationship, holding the other person at a more comfortable distance.

If you fear being suffocated or engulfed in relationships, you may develop the pattern of hiding from those close to you. The childhood belief here is that, "The only way I can have something all my own is by withholding it from the world." The "something" can be as simple as a favorite seashell or as complex as the right to choose a career.

Gil is a good example of this dynamic. A pleasant-looking cab driver who is gay, Gil enjoyed watching sexually explicit videotapes, and had developed a large collection of them. But he kept this hobby a secret from everyone, and continued hiding it when his lover David moved in.

Although Gil admitted he had no reason to fear David's judgment about it, he was unwilling to take the risk. "What will I do," asked Gil, "if he's turned off?" He refused to take such a chance, even though the two of them had enjoyed X-rated films at theatres together several times.

Gil's decision to keep this a secret was an effective way of controlling the distance in the relationship. His secrecy resulted in his feeling alone, separate from David, guilty, and even resentful. It limited the quality of their sex together. And while none of this felt good, the situation did feel safer, in an odd way.

"Look, the bottom line is just me," he said once. "Why take chances on someone else's feelings? I know I can count on me, and I'd rather not worry about other people making my life complicated."

Acting out feelings

One way our unconscious attempts to help us survive is by instructing us to hold back from expressing certain feelings directly. Expressing them *indirectly* through actions is called *acting out.*

The most common feeling that people act out through secrecy is anger. The infantile part of us fears we will be abandoned or destroyed if we express this directly, so we express it covertly. We do this through the effects that sexual secrets have, such as hurting someone or breaking an agreement. Such effects subtly gratify the anger that our unconscious believes is too dangerous to express directly. Other feelings that we sometimes act out through sexual secrecy include fear, grief, jealousy, despair, and competitiveness.

Let's look at an illustration of how acting out can be an unconscious solution to the conflict between needing and fearing closeness. The speaker is a struggling actress I'll call Lynette, a tall woman who recently came to see me about her "endless frustrations." During out third session, she described an incident from the previous weekend.

"My husband, Karl, and I were out shopping together, and I ran into an old friend named Jay. We all got along nicely; in fact, we sat for almost an hour having coffee. Later, Karl asked how I knew Jay, and I made up a story about acting classes."

I nodded and said nothing. Lynette continued: "The truth is that Jay and I used to sleep together before I married Karl. I feel guilty about having lied, but I just wasn't prepared to tell the truth."

When I asked why, Lynette had several logical reasons. But there was very little feeling in her voice until she added, with a shrug, "Besides, Karl is no angel. Ask him about the teller who used to work at our bank's merchant window. Or the one who works there now, for that matter."

Suddenly Lynette's voice had life, so I pursued this. Apparently she felt that Karl had occasional affairs with other women. Had she tried to work out her resentment about this with Karl before? "Yes," she said with a trace of bitterness. She had confronted him with her suspicions, but never received much satisfaction. "He's always saying how he wants me to be happy, but when I'd tell him what was bothering me, he'd become impatient. Finally I just figured it was a waste of time."

Noting this, I moved on to Lynette's other relationships. After asking a few questions, I saw that she had this same sense of powerlessness and unimportance with her father, first husband, and boss. And with her previous therapist too. What was this pattern about?

"You get mad at people, they can't handle it," she said at one point. "No one wants to know what you *really* think, no matter what they say. I've made that mistake before, and I'll never do it again." Lynette was working hard to survive by burying her anger, but it had to go somewhere. How convenient to have sexual secrets, such as the one about Jay, with which to humiliate Karl and feel she had the upper hand.

The problem here isn't Lynette's lying, it's her belief that certain feelings endanger closeness. Once Lynette works that out—by resolving her leftover fears about being abandoned—she'll be able to make more rational decisions about how to relate to those she cares about. Actually, that's the focus of her therapy at this time.

Acting out is not usually a productive compromise. Although you feel better for a moment, you virtually guarantee that the problem that is bothering you will come back later.

Fulfilling script demands

The idea that each of us follows personal life scripts was developed by Dr. Eric Berne in the early 1960s. These scripts, according to the theories of his Transactional Analysis, come from decisions we make early in childhood. Designed to help us survive, those decisions lead to adult styles and beliefs that restrict our ability to live flexible, free lives, responsive to the opportunities and demands of the moment.

No one consciously chooses to go along with a script. In fact, it is rare to have even an inkling of what your scripts are. Yet, aware or not, we make choices throughout our lives that fulfill the roles laid out in these scripts.

Everyone is familiar with the folk wisdom that names many common scripts: the Peter Pan, who won't grow up; the Love Addict, who will put up with anything rather than be alone; the Angry Young Man, who would rather criticize than be nurtured. Let's look at some scripts that can be fulfilled by sexual secrets:

- "I'm not completely loveable, and never will be."
- "I'm a bad person."
- "I'm always being victimized or abused by those around me."
- "I must protect people who hurt me."
- "It's my job to keep peace and make sure no one's upset."
- "Women don't enjoy sex."
- "Men and women are never sexually compatible."
- "Men/women will love me for my mind but be bored with my looks."

- "For gay people, sex will always be complicated."
- "I will die heroically."
- "I'm not important enough for anyone to care about."

In chapters 4 to 7, we will look at dozens of sexual secrets that help fulfill each of these scripts. For now, let's look at an example of how scripts and secrets are connected.

Here is a very common script that people often play out in non-sexual ways. In the case that follows, it was played out sexually.

> Script: "I've always got some kind of emotional problem—life would be empty without one."
> Secret: "I have herpes."

Maurice, a stocky man with striking blue eyes, has had herpes for six years. Through a combination of medication and group therapy, he has brought it under control. Now Maurice has only one or two outbreaks per year.

Nevertheless, the sandy-haired engineer hides his condition from his sexual partners, claiming to be "just not in the mood" when he is contagious. Given the chance, any of his steady girlfriends over the years might have simply accepted the fact of his herpes. They could have gone for joint counseling, if necessary, or specifically focused on "safer sex."

But Maurice is stuck on his herpes. He *needs* to be, because a serious relationship without a disturbing problem is too scary for him. It makes him feel vulnerable, makes him feel the relationship is about to overwhelm and carry him away, and that he has no anchor.

By keeping the herpes a secret, Maurice makes it a problem. This allows him to participate in a relationship with less fear—to "survive." And it allows him to extend his belief in the myth surrounding his script, which is, "If I could only clear up my problem, life could be great."

It's hard for us to see our own scripts because we're inside them. Still, you can ask yourself about the themes in your life. What seems inevitable? What is your "fate"? What were you born for? What are your family's myths about you?

THE ILLUSION—AND ITS PRICE

Sexual secrecy does appear to make the world of relationships safer, but this sense of safety is an illusion. Since the threat of annihilation is actually in the past, there is nothing you can do in the present to make you safer back then.

The illusion of safety carries a high price tag. Although sexual secrecy cannot change the childhood experiences that felt so threatening, the results of pursuing childhood safety through adult secrecy does have powerful, unintended effects.

The sense you get from secret-keeping isn't real power; it's *pseudo-power*. That is, you give up the drive to be accepted as okay—and instead, you settle for not being attacked (by yourself or others) for not being okay.

Maurice has given up on the possibility of being accepted as okay, supposedly because he has herpes. Instead, he settles for not being attacked or rejected because of his herpes. He does this by hiding the condition.

Strategies that tap pseudo-power often involve withholding: not telling a partner how you like to be stimulated, or what turns you off. A *truly* powerful approach is taking the initiative: "I'd like us to make my orgasm more of a priority. How could we do that?"

Sexual secrecy also seems valuable as a way of creating and controlling emotional distance in relationships. Once you restrict closeness, however, it cannot always flourish fully again. Intimacy is the product of trust, of the willingness to risk and explore *with* another person. Once one partner asserts control over that process, it stops being mutual. Closeness may not grow any further until circumstances change.

Acting out feelings through sexual secrecy can be gratifying. But this keeps you from communicating effectively, and from having the kind of power you need to change a painful situation. This is the problem with acting out survival fears: you feel better in the short run but guarantee that you'll feel bad again soon. Ironically, by keeping sexual secrets we create the very situations we most fear.

Some relationships, unfortunately, discourage the direct expression of feelings. There are marriages that need a weak or frightened partner in order to be stable. Beliefs like "I can't make it on my own" help these relationships last, but they stunt the growth of the participants.

In such cases, rebellion—through sexual secrecy—is a way for the person who plays the weak and frightened role to act out anger and shame. Unfortunately, you can be so caught up in survival issues that you fail to see their disastrous long-term effects.

Finally, using sexual secrecy to fulfill childhood scripts is very costly. As discussed, scripts emerge as the mind grapples with a single goal: preventing childhood pain. So scripts specifically ignore the needs of contemporary, adult situations.

Such scripts are like an aunt who wants to protect her niece from rowdy boys who are only interested in "one thing." The trouble is, the niece is now thirty, and wants to meet a good man. If she listens to her aunt, she never will. As with acting out, the problem with fulfilling scripts is that it feels good at the moment, but prevents happiness in the long run.

Your willingness to look at the many illusions surrounding sexual secrecy, and their costs, is a crucial step toward improving your sexual satisfaction and relationship. Anyone willing to do that will be rewarded by a deeper, more satisfying relationship.

Given the unconscious fear many of us have about sexuality and relationships, secrecy looks like an attractive way to avoid the judgments and unpredictable attacks we anticipate from those we allow close to us.

And so we experience the value of secrecy. It is a way of acting out feelings that seem dangerous, of creating distance, of seizing what *feels* like power but really isn't, and of fulfilling old, outdated psychological scripts.

Secrecy makes relationships seem safer by reducing the amount of trust and commitment we need in order to participate in them. Secrecy lets us create a private world within our relationships, allowing us to avoid our own uncomfortable feelings.

Unexamined, the costs of these wonderful advantages seem low. This is especially true if you work them into your personality, reinforcing whatever tendencies you have toward being dour, flighty, snide, resigned, and so on.

The truth, of course, is that the costs of secrecy's apparent value are high. But given the dilemma we humans find ourselves in—needing people in order to survive, and fearing that that need will destroy us—this is a difficult truth to hear.

It's difficult to tell a starving child that the food she has found is toxic. Perhaps more to the point, it's difficult to tell a man who is sure he's being chased that the car he's trying to escape in has a tire about to blow out.

EPILOGUE: EROTIC DISTANCE

According to some sexologists, there is one other value offered by sexual secrecy. It creates mystery, they say, which legitimately enriches a sexual relationship. While this isn't an idea that I necessarily believe, it is interesting to consider.

Champions of this theory of "erotic distance," such as psychologists Jack Morin, Robert Stoller, and C.A. Tripp, tend to see two phases of relationships. The first is the can't-get-enough-of-you, everything-makes-me-lustful stage, which Dorothy Tennov calls "limerance." During this phase, nothing special is required to maintain sexual interest.

Limerance inevitably wears off, however, and when it does, says Morin, "Some people intuitively know how to keep the passion up. They use a variety of ways to create a special psychological distance, some erotic barrier to sexual intimacy." It is the very challenge of overcoming such barriers, claim these theorists, that keeps sex hot over time.

"Sexual secrecy," claims Morin, "can be one form of maintaining that important barrier. It can also contribute to the feeling that you desire something naughty or forbidden, which also turns some people on."

As I say, I am not comfortable with this theory. However, let's say for a moment that it is accurate. The question is, can we take charge of this dynamic and operate it in a beneficial way? Or must we be at the mercy of it, destined to act it out self-destructively?

If sexual secrets are "necessary" to keep sex exciting, we should attempt to minimize their negative impact. Thus, use secrets that:

- Don't involve your resentments
- Put you in a playful mood when you think about them
- Won't hurt your partner if/when revealed
- Don't challenge the fundamental connection of the partnership
- Don't hit upon a partner's special insecurity

Examples of secrets that you might keep from your partner include any special trick that you use to pleasure him or her, a favorite fantasy, or a private ritual you use to turn yourself on.

Sexual secrets, in some ways, are like other secrets. Sexuality, however, is *not* like other things for most of us. Few other cultures in history have given it as much emotional charge as ours.

Thus, if sexuality is the issue we feel guilty and vulnerable about, the result is tremendous anxiety and fear. Sexual secrets can easily look like the key to survival. To be free in adulthood, we must put our childhood fears to rest once and for all. The good news is that we do *not* have to ransom our sexuality to do so.

PART II

COMMON
SEXUAL
SECRETS

Sexually, are you normal?

If I had to guess, I'd say yes. And that's without knowing how often you have sex, whom you do it with, how well you do it, or even what you do.

Surprised?

Almost everyone seems to wonder if they're sexually normal. When it comes to other activities, of course, we know how we measure up. For example, we watch other people eat, drive, buy clothes, make phone calls, and discipline their children. We can compare ourselves to these strangers, and usually we decide that we're okay.

But sex? Whom are you going to watch? Whom can you talk to? Besides, seriously talking about sex with others can be very frustrating. As a result, we compare ourselves to media images of classic beauty, self-confidence, perfect functioning, dependable desire—and plenty of time to enjoy it all. We always fall short by comparison.

In therapy sessions, on the lecture circuit, and in my mail, people ask me for measurements of sexual normalcy—which I generally refuse to give. Instead of using numbers, I'd rather you decide that you're sexually normal based on a warm sense of self-acceptance. One of my main reasons for writing this book is to give you information, guidelines, and encouragement for accepting yourself.

Let's start with a simple checklist that illustrates the wide range of sexually normal behavior. You are *not* abnormal, just because you:

- Have sex once a day, or once every three months
- Have only one sex partner in a lifetime, or a dozen different ones each year
- Masturbate every day, or not at all—regardless of marital status
- Think about someone other than your partner during sex—even someone completely off-limits
- Never fantasize about others
- Acquire a sexually transmitted disease
- Prefer oral or manual sex to intercourse, or vice versa
- Enjoy many different positions, or the same routine every time
- Are ashamed of your body, or proud of it
- Feel excited or depressed about the sexual changes aging brings, or not notice any changes
- Experience your sexual preferences and feelings change during the course of a month, or a year
- Have erection or orgasm problems
- Find it difficult to discuss your feelings or preferences, even with the person to whom you are closest
- Have been victimized through rape, forced sex, or childhood molestation
- Wonder if you're normal

It doesn't matter where on this list you locate yourself. The fact that you find yourself here at all is what's important. We all have our favorite colors, ice cream flavors, and TV shows, preferences we accept without question. It would be nice to accept our own—and others'—sexual preferences as easily.

Why does normalcy rate its own discussion? Because concerns about normalcy lie behind much of the secrecy discussed in the following chapters. There would be less anguish in today's world if more people knew they were sexually normal.

ABOUT CASE STUDIES

Therapy is a wonderful tool for helping people understand themselves and grow beyond their present limits. Clients gain insight into the most basic parts of human personality. They become more familiar and comfortable with their own emotions, including fear, anger, love, sadness, joy, and guilt.

Being in therapy is not like sitting in a classroom. Instead of lecturing people, therapists help them experience the meaning of their behavior and relationships. Similarly, instead of simply telling you what people have learned, I'm going to help you discover it with them. That's the value of case studies.

Because these stories are relatively brief, the process may seem like magic. Remember, however, that each case represents months—occasionally years—of hard work. At times that work is boring, frustrating, or painful. Success in therapy usually occurs slowly. It did not happen overnight for any of the people you will meet in the next chapters.

Every person whose story you read here is "normal." They all entered therapy because they wanted more from life. The old idea that therapy is only for sick people is obsolete and inaccurate. Rest assured that these case studies do not violate anyone's confidentiality. Details of the cases have been altered, and composites have been created from similar cases.

Don't judge the people in these stories. Love them, as I urge you to love yourself. Learn from their pain and joy. We're all alone in this together, you know.

4

AROUSAL
AND RESPONSE

Orgasm: the perfect compromise between love and death.
— ROBERT BAK

By the time we are adults, the Secrecy Imperative has taken its toll. We think of our incestuous fantasies, our curiosity about others' bodies, our joyful desire to masturbate, and the rest of our sexuality as bad, needing to be controlled.

In an attempt to protect ourselves from this "bad" part, we unconsciously reject it or split it off from the rest of our psyche. This is the opposite of the wholeness and self-acceptance that define mental health. Although it is painful to disown any part of ourselves, it usually feels absolutely necessary. "If you don't control that nasty sexuality," says your inner voice, "it will control you."

That's why we will do virtually anything to protect ourselves from this "bad" part. We will even sacrifice our self-respect, or live without intimacy.

Gaining distance from your "dangerous" sexuality is not something you can do once and forget about; it's a lifelong job. You may briefly succeed in chasing away sexual thoughts and feelings, but they will always be on the brink of pushing their way back into your awareness. For someone who is sure that these sexual images are bad, round-the-clock mental vigilance is needed.

One way most people try to exercise this discipline is by following social norms defining acceptable sexual behavior. In effect, we mentally chaperone ourselves. Adjectives such as "polite," "ladylike," "respectable," and "normal" describe such behavior. All other kinds of sex, such as non-marital, non-intercourse, or non-reproductive are denigrated as dirty, animal-like, unnatural, or sinful.

Consider a thirty-nine-year-old machinist who came to see me several months ago. Jack put a lot of energy into protecting himself and his community from "sexual perversion." He acted as if it were a contagious disease, and that he was especially vulnerable.

Jack was against school sex education because he felt it encouraged kids to have sex. He wanted homosexuals jailed or "cured" so they couldn't seduce heterosexuals. He tried to stop the private rental of X-rated videos so that people would not get "sick ideas" about lovemaking. And he believed only married couples should have access to contraception.

Jack's deep wish to restrict other people's sexual expression was a statement about himself. He was clearly afraid of the power of sexuality—particularly his own. To deal with his fear he had, unconsciously, made this dangerous sexuality into an external object. Because this "object" came from within himself, he saw the danger everywhere.

Jack reminds me of an Indian fable I like very much: There once was a man who was so displeased by the sight of his own shadow that he determined to be rid of it forever. He commenced to run, but no matter how fast he went, he could not get away from it. So he ran, faster and faster. Finally, the constant running so exhausted the man that he dropped dead.

He did not realize that if only he had stopped running and had sat down under a tree, his shadow would have disappeared.

A powerful interest in sexuality was Jack's secret, which he hid even from himself. Rather than become aware of his fear, confront it, and deal with it, he became attached to distorted theories about sex and its expression. He felt safest in groups of people who agreed with him, where everyone else was loudly denying *their* powerful sexuality, too. Together they went around trying to destroy the sexual enemy "out there."

I didn't try to talk Jack out of his opinions. Instead, I helped him become aware of the unconscious belief that a vital part of him was bad. Until he changed that belief, he would see the devil lurking everywhere. You can't, after all, run away from your shadow.

"PROPER" SEXUAL CONDUCT

Ours is a society of great diversity, and individual tastes vary. Still, you are familiar with our culture's definition of normal sexual conduct:

- Penis-vagina intercourse, missionary position
- Between two people, one male, one female, who love each other
- Initiated by the male
- Male has an instant, firm erection
- The woman is ladylike (not too sweaty, noisy, or enthusiastic)
- She lubricates copiously
- Sex is simple and does not require any discussion
- The woman climaxes easily
- The man climaxes soon after she does

This ideal is as much a part of our heritage as Babe Ruth, Paul Bunyan, and Betsy Ross. According to surveys, however, most of us don't fit this mold of "proper" arousal and response. A 1975 *Redbook* magazine sexuality study reported that 85 percent of its married readers engaged in cunnilingus, and that 43 percent had had anal sex.

Sad to say, many people feel compelled to withhold information about their preferences from their partners or even themselves. Why? Because of fear that they'll be rejected for enjoying sex the "wrong way." It's a dreadful reminder from childhood. In this adult version, our partner is the parent and we're the child. Thus, the childhood strategy seems safest: when in doubt, hide the truth.

Unfortunately, this leaves you feeling guilty, fearing discovery, and knowing you're not loved for your true self. So publicly, we profess the faith of straight sex. But every modern study of sexual behavior shows that in private, people do quite varied things. Hence, the old saying: "What I like is variety. What you like is kinky. What they like is perverse."

For example, few people are willing to say that erotic films and books should not be suppressed; no one wants to be accused of favoring pornography. And yet, erotica is a billion-dollar industry. It couldn't exist with only a few thousand demented customers. Tens of millions of normal people consume erotica.

Adult bookstore owners have been saying for years that their customers are you and me. But, fearing punishment, no one wants to admit it. Most of us aren't adult enough to seize the power to make our own sexual judgments and decisions. We're still masturbating in the bathroom, hiding from Mommy.

COMMON SECRETS

Let us now turn to some common sexual secrets about arousal and response: what turns us on, and how we react to being turned on. The areas of secrecy include preferences, conditions, sex drive, our bodies, sexual dysfunctions, and "You don't really turn me on."

Preferences

One of the most prevalent secrets involves the kinds of sexual stimulation people like. In a culture that defines the "right way" so narrowly, it isn't surprising that so many common preferences are considered deviant. Just what we need—another reason to feel ashamed about our sexuality.

For example, more than half of American women say they prefer clitoral to vaginal stimulation for climaxing, according to studies by Shere Hite and Lonnie Barbach. Yet many men and women, misled by Freudian psychology, romance literature, and traditional male folk wisdom, find this common preference strange and undesirable.

How exasperating is this cultural bias? Barbach notes in her lectures that, "Women are as frustrated by this as men would be if they knew they were supposed to reach orgasm by having their testicles rubbed."

Because intercourse doesn't usually provide enough clitoral stimulation, many women prefer to climax from oral or manual sex. Some men prefer making love this way too, because it requires less energy, produces more intense sensations, and involves less performance pressure. Yet, men and women keep this and other preferences secret, and come to therapy worried about them.

Dave did just that. Dave was a healthy, middle-aged man who enjoyed sex. He functioned just fine, but his preference for fellatio over intercourse troubled him. His worry led him to seek treatment.

"Perhaps deep down, I'm gay," he said anxiously during our first session. "God, I hope not. I certainly don't want anyone else to think that. Besides, how do you know that a woman isn't resenting oral sex, but doing it anyway?" Understandably, Dave never asked for oral sex, and he hesitated to accept a woman doing it spontaneously. He said that the secrecy made him feel like a fraud. Periodically, he'd stop dating altogether. Sexuality became a lonely conflict between pleasure, frustration, and worry.

After two sessions, it was clear that Dave didn't have any special problems with intimacy. What he needed most was reassurance that he was normal. I thought the *Hite Report* would help. "Almost all [the 7,000 interviewed] men said that they enjoyed fellatio tremendously," it says. One man even wrote, "A loving and ardent mouth is more stimulating and exciting than a vagina any day."

I convinced Dave to ask a few women friends how they felt about fellatio. Three of the four he asked assured him that they enjoyed it. He now believes that his interest is "normal," that he can trust himself, and that he no longer needs to be secretive about his preference.

Women present this kind of situation in therapy as frequently as men. A thirty-year-old secretary named Marie was referred to me by her physician. Marie was worried because she preferred stimulation of her clitoris far more than other forms of sex.

Marie had intercourse mostly to please her husband, Don. Although she enjoyed the closeness, she usually felt frustrated afterward. She encouraged Don to "do more," but she felt she couldn't come out and "admit" her need. Without an explicit discussion, they couldn't get in sync.

What troubled Marie most was sneaking away to the bathroom after intercourse to masturbate. Because she was usually very aroused, orgasm only took a minute. But the pleasure was mixed with other feelings: anger at her husband for not satisfying her, guilt about needing "a hand job" and having one without him, and fear that he would find out and feel rejected.

After only two therapy sessions, Marie decided to "come out" to Don. As she told me a few days later, "It was just as bad as I feared. He was insulted and we fought bitterly."

In the weeks that followed, Marie and Don argued about sex often. They blamed each other, dug up old wounds, and accused each other of being inadequate. "But finally I realized that I'd had enough," she told me one day. "I did some soul-searching. I asked Don, 'Aren't I still the same loving wife that I've always been? I have a simple sexual need, and I won't apologize for it.' "

That's when Marie and Don started marital counseling. It was clear that more than a sexual problem, they had a power problem. Marie's honesty had forced it into the open, and there would be no going back. She and Don are still having rough times, but their conflicts have changed. They have more respect for each other, and are aiming for a new kind of honesty. If they can attain this honesty, they'll be closer than ever before.

Conditions

As therapist Bernie Zilbergeld notes in his wonderful book *Male Sexuality,* each of us has unique, individual conditions for satisfying sex. Despite what we learn from romance novels and James Bond films, simply having a willing partner is not enough. Yet many people believe that when it comes to sexual desire and satisfaction, they should be like those automated bank tellers—available and operating twenty-four hours a day.

In real life, the variety of people's requirements for enjoyable sex is endless. Examples include privacy, closeness, a youthful partner, a sense of rule-breaking, and reliable contraception.

"A condition," Zilbergeld says in *Male Sexuality,* is "anything that makes you more relaxed, comfortable, confident, and open to your sexual experience." It's something that helps "clear your nervous system of unnecessary clutter, leaving it open to receive and transmit sexual messages" in satisfying ways. "When sex doesn't work out the way we like, we are too ready to assume that something is wrong with us, rather than with the situation."

Believing we shouldn't have conditions, we hide them. Conditions are another aspect of sexuality that many people keep secret. Some conditions involve the absence of particular turn-offs. For different people, these might include being teased about their body shape or weight, a sense of being rushed, the smell of cigarettes, a partner's mechanical technique. One of my own conditions—I admit it!—is no country music.

Since sex without our conditions being met can be scary, boring, frustrating, or unpleasant, why do we so often agree to have sex without them? Usually because we don't believe others will accept our conditions—because we don't accept them ourselves. The issue makes me think of Simon, a boutique owner I worked with a few years ago.

"I'm crazy about this new girl," he told me. "She's very pretty, and she likes me." So why, he asked, was he losing interest during their lovemaking?

I asked if there were any problems outside of bed. "Oh, she likes to drink," he replied. "In fact, she likes me to drink, too. Says it makes her feel sexy." And how did he feel about it? "Oh, I don't love it," he said, "but it's okay, I guess." It was one of those answers that rings a bell in a therapist's mind; I decided to hang on to it for the time being.

The following week Simon was back. "We made love again," he said as soon as he sat down. "And halfway through, the same damn thing happened. What's wrong with me?"

I asked Simon to close his eyes and visualize the situation. What did he hear, smell, feel, and taste?

"Gloria's skin," he smiled. "It feels so soft. And music. We both like cello music. Now she's whispering to me." I saw him wrinkle his nose. "Anything wrong?" I asked. "No," he said quickly, but under his breath I heard something. "What is it?" I asked again.

"Just the booze," he said, with a trace of anger. "Why does she have to spoil it with the booze?" It was clear that Simon hated the smell of alcohol on Gloria's breath. He said he had mentioned it to her once or twice, had gotten no response, and had dropped it.

During our session, Simon realized that he disliked Gloria smelling of alcohol partly because it reminded him of his childhood, when he was cared for by an inept, alcoholic grandfather. Rather than confront Gloria, however, Simon decided to swallow his discomfort.

"I'm the one who should change," he said stoically. "This is a stupid thing to get upset about. Besides," he added quietly, "what if she refuses to change?"

This, of course, was what the secret-keeping was about, and what our therapy began to focus on.

Simon chose to stay on the very difficult path of denying, and therefore hiding, one of his most important conditions. His resentment showed itself, indirectly, in his wavering libido. I think larger problems lie ahead for him.

Concern about the reasonableness of a condition is just another version of the most common sexual concern: "Am I normal?" I believe that most simple conditions that don't involve coercion or pain are both common and harmless.

Sex drive

Many people hide the true nature of their sex drive, believing themselves abnormal. According to Shere Hite, "There is a great deal of anxiety on the part of most men [surveyed] about how often they have intercourse." In fact, "Many men are fairly sure that they should be having it more often than they are."

Since men are supposed to want sex more than women, they frequently hide what they consider a too low desire. They may initiate sex when they don't really want it. Instead of just politely refusing, they will pick a fight, or say they are tired, or get involved in TV or reading, or wait until their partner is asleep before going to bed. As a long-term, unconscious solution, these men often get a second job, new civic responsibilities, or a new hobby.

Women, on the other hand, more often hide a too high desire. They may go to therapy to get "fixed," or masturbate in the attempt to decrease their interest, or continually experiment with lingerie and perfume to get their partner aroused. How different these women's lives would be if they simply admitted the truth about their sex drive and worked with their mates to find a reasonable compromise.

The subject reminds me of an incident that happened in Los Angeles a few years back. I was the guest on a call-in radio show, and a listener asked me to define "nymphomaniac." "Sexual labels are arbitrary and relative," I told him. "Many people think that a nymphomaniac is any woman who wants sex one more time than her partner."

While people often hide or repress their true sex drive out of fear of rejection, there is another reason. You may be one of those who, convinced that your sexuality is bad, fear that "giving in" to it will result in its taking over, and that, overpowered by lust, you'll want sex all the time. A woman recently referred to me by a social worker turned out to fit that description.

Rachel was a short woman with huge blue eyes who had an extremely low sexual desire. "I love my husband," she said, "but I just don't want sex with him very much." The problem had started a year ago after a long vacation during which they had had sex every day. What was it about the intense pleasure that had dampened her pilot light?

Eventually, we started discussing her adolescence. "My parents were extreme workaholics, with very little time for me," she recalled. "They didn't care much about my schoolwork or friends or anything. At fifteen I went all the way with a college guy I was dating. The ecstatic look on his face when he came thrilled me. When he said he loved me I just melted."

"That year, I slept with most of his friends," she continued. "I became hooked on this new drug of making men go wild, and I developed quite a reputation. But by the time I was twenty I felt old. I began to realize that these guys didn't care about me, that they had just used me. In my own way, I suppose, I had used them too. A year later I met Lee, the first decent guy I ever knew. I married him as fast as I could, and then we left the state."

Unconsciously, Rachel believed that this five-year period of high sexual activity was her true nature. She had spent the years since fearing that the "madness" of uncontrolled sexual interest would return, get hold of her, and ruin her life. Feeling safe in her new marriage, she was slowly working out a satisfying sexual arrangement with Lee—until the vacation.

I asked if Lee knew about the "wild days." Some, she replied quietly, but not much. She was afraid that if he found out he'd be upset. "I don't like to think about it. That would almost be like inviting it back," she said.

Here, then, was the secret: "I've been bad." And the fear: "I'm afraid Lee will judge me and then leave me." The sexually active vacation had restimulated all the old fears about getting out of control. Her subsequent loss of desire was an unconscious way of coping with those fears.

I gently encouraged Rachel to accept the way she had handled a difficult childhood. Some teens, I told her, develop alcohol, theft, or school problems to cope with the lack of parental attention. Sex had been her ingenious, if accidental, solution.

Once Rachel began to accept that she wasn't bad, she became less afraid that Lee would judge her. More important, she became less afraid of losing control of her sexuality. She soon decided to ask Lee to come in with her for a joint session so she could share her fears with him. That was three months ago. Today, Rachel enjoys sex as an exciting, intimate experience.

My body

In some ways, body features are the most universally kept sexual secret. All of us, particularly women, have moments of wanting to hide our bodies. Yet few people are able to talk with others about this and grow beyond it.

Much of the problem stems from our modern culture's obsession with physical beauty. Most of us spend more time improving our body's appearance than we spend improving our health. Not surprisingly, some Americans develop disorders such as anorexia and bulimia, in which distorted self-image leads to dangerous self-starvation.

Predictably, Americans are also in love with plastic surgery. To improve our beauty, this billion-dollar industry offers many common procedures, such as breast enlargement, that are frequently disastrous and even disabling.

The shame you feel about your body is probably most acute before or during sexual encounters. You may be embarrassed about scars, too little or too much hair, or what you believe are ugly genitalia. Fully one-half of the letters sent to my column in *Men's Guide to Fashion* express concern about penis size or shape. From what most women say, you'd think that breasts come in only two sizes: too large and too small.

According to a 1987 *Redbook* survey, "The single factor most responsible for whatever sexual inhibitions today's women feel . . . is insecurity about physical appearance. Fully 41 percent [of 26,000 respondents] said that these feelings prevent them from freely expressing their sexuality."

Sexual secret-keeping resulting from body shame drains our energy and creativity. People who keep such secrets often want the lights off during sex, and may refuse to make love in positions they feel are unflattering. Sometimes they prohibit certain kinds of touching that might reveal their secret.

The secret can be almost anything: a scar, extremely small breasts, a hairy backside, inverted nipples, small testicles. Our tendency to feel ashamed of normal variations in body features is quite impressive. And quite unfortunate.

One of the many people with this kind of shame is Sandy, an intelligent woman who is about thirty pounds overweight. She came to me because she had trouble reaching orgasm with a partner. When I asked about a typical sexual encounter, this is what she said:

"First of all, I won't get on top, even though that is really my favorite position. I don't want anyone seeing how much my breasts sag. Other positions are out, too—doing it from behind, for example, because my butt is huge and I know any guy would be turned off.

"Once I decide to make love with someone, I suggest my house. I keep lots of candles by the bed, so the lighting is soft, more flattering. I discourage men from touching my belly or thighs. It feels good to *me,* but they're, you know, squishy, flabby. It's just too embarrassing.

"Although I feel okay about the whole thing most of the time," Sandy continued, "sometimes I feel like a second-class citizen. I get angry at men for being so prejudiced, and then I get angry at myself for caring so much. And of course, it's frustrating to get excited and then not come. Sometimes I worry that that turns men off also. What the hell, when it's too much I just stop dating for a month or two. Then I forget the bad feelings, and I get back into it."

Although Sandy likes sex, a big part of lovemaking involves monitoring her body's attractiveness. Her attention is divided between enjoying sex and hiding her body. The conflict between these activities made orgasm difficult for her, while her rules about touching prevented the stimulation she needed. No wonder she couldn't climax with a partner.

Sandy's anger about feeling lonely and demeaned is yet another obstacle to satisfaction. It's understandable; Sandy feels out of control. Her sexual secrecy, in dictating her behavior, has rendered her powerless.

Occasionally, a therapist will joke good-naturedly about working with a tougher version of this case. One colleague used to say that he knew a couple who made love only during total eclipses of the sun. That's because they wouldn't take their clothes off unless it was dark everywhere in the world.

Other common secrets about our bodies include:

- I'm sterile (and I know you want children, so I'm not going to tell you right now)
- I have herpes or some other STD (it's under control right now, but I'm afraid you would reject me if I told you)
- I'm a woman who climaxes very easily, and/or has multiple orgasms (and I'm afraid you'd be intimidated or judgmental if you knew)
- I'm afraid to make love without a few drinks first

Sexual dysfunction

According to pioneer sexologists Masters and Johnson, some forty million Americans are sexually dissatisfied. Ideally, such a widespread problem would be freely discussed, but in this puritanical society, it isn't so. On the contrary, having a sexual problem or concern is one of the most common sexual secrets.

In our media-dominated era, sexual dysfunction carries a sort of moral blemish, the way alcoholism and divorce once did (and still do in some places). Thus, people often choose to hide a sexual problem from their partners, from professionals who might help them, and even, through denial, rationalization, and projection, from themselves.

Forty-four-year-old William was a bus driver with such a dilemma. "About a year ago I lost my erection in the middle of lovemaking, for the first time. It didn't bother me that much, but when it happened again the next night, I got nervous," he told me.

"Both of my main girlfriends were leaving town to take better jobs about then, so I was soon back in circulation, as they say. In the first few weeks I met a couple of new women, so I was in business. But I had the impotence a couple more times, and that did it. No more lovemaking, I decided, until I get this fixed."

I pondered the probability that his girlfriends' departure helped cause the original erectile problem, but I said nothing. I wanted to hear the story William's way, without interruption.

William fidgeted a bit and went on. "I became pretty creative at excuses—early day with my kid tomorrow, too much to drink, got a lot on my mind, too upset by the movie we just saw. It was lonely, but better than admitting I had a sex problem.

"I've seen a few doctors," he concluded, "but they can't seem to fix me. I'm pretty discouraged right now. And, of course, I don't feel I can hold on to a woman indefinitely without sex."

William's was the kind of case that reminds me of the difference between anxiety and panic. Anxiety is what you feel the first time you can't get an erection twice. Panic is what you feel the second time you can't get an erection once. William had only been anxious for a few days when he went straight to panic.

Like most of us, William could manage for a long time without intercourse. But the lack of touching and affection troubled him a great deal. William also felt very bad about fooling the women he dated.

This guilt and his constant monitoring of potentially "dangerous" situations kept him from making emotional contact with women. Sadly, his feelings prevented him from discovering that there were women who would have accepted him just as he was. Sharing his secret would have been a calculated risk, but it could have resulted in the nurturing William needed so badly.

Judgments and criticism

A surprisingly large number of people have strong criticisms of the way their partners make love. Examples of these judgments include:

- "You don't really turn me on."
- "You're lousy in bed."
- "I don't like what we do."

In a way, unexpressed criticisms like these are the ultimate sexual secret. Since it intimately involves your mate's self-concept, sharing this secret really tests a relationship.

And yet, concealing sexual judgments is common. Shere Hite reports that many men wish their partners would fellate them differently, but say nothing. Dozens of writers, including Anais Nin, attest to women's reluctance to discuss the way their partners make love.

Perhaps you keep this secret because:

- You're not supposed to know what good sex is
- You don't want to upset your partner
- You're not sure you deserve good sex
- You don't want to fight
- You're not aware that sex can be really satisfying or comfortable
- It lets you hold onto the fantasy that things will change in the future

The woman in the next case history had several of these reasons for keeping her secret.

Lynn and Claude were a pleasant, affluent couple in their late thirties who obviously loved each other. They appeared to "have it all"—money, careers, a beautiful child. But they just couldn't seem to find time for lovemaking. He had an important corporate position, and also supervised the maid and gardener. She had a busy law practice, was raising their child, and performed in a local orchestra.

Interestingly, they both agreed that Claude was the sex expert in the marriage. "He's had lots of experience," said Lynn. Claude obviously enjoyed this respect.

In private, however, Lynn added some interesting detail. She was not really satisfied with Claude's lovemaking. "But I can't criticize it," she explained. "He knows a lot more about sex than I do. I just need to get with it a little more. I'll come around eventually."

I asked her to visualize a perfect sexual encounter with a stranger: the pace, activities, and feelings. The scene she described was quite different from her routine with Claude. When I pointed this out, Lynn became thoughtful. Then she understood. "It's not up to me to fit in with his 'expertise,'" she suddenly exclaimed. "It's up to him to do what I like!"

Which meant, of course, that she would have to explain her dissatisfaction and desire for change. This meant dethroning Claude as the expert, and establishing herself as a co-expert. Lynn was understandably hesitant because doing so would definitely change the balance of power in the rest of their marriage. But she decided to tell the truth so she could enjoy sex more and feel closer to Claude. It wasn't easy, but it worked.

The 1975 *Redbook* study noted a dramatic correlation. The more a woman discusses her sexual feelings with her husband, the more likely she is to report her sex life as "good" or "very good."

As Lynn herself put it recently, "Nobody *chooses* to frustrate you in bed. They may not change if you discuss your true needs, but they certainly won't change if you stay quiet about it."

Lynn understands the dynamics fairly well. She is still, however, hesitant to act. Which is probably how most of us feel about the secrets in this chapter. After all, the more closely we identify with one of our secrets, the more we hesitate to reveal it. And it's difficult to imagine anything that could be more individual, more "us," than our arousal and response patterns.

In the next chapter, we'll look at another group of sexual secrets: fantasies and feelings.

5

FANTASIES AND FEELINGS

The conscious mind allows itself to be trained like a parrot, but the unconscious mind does not—which is why St. Augustine thanked God for not making him responsible for his dreams.

—CARL JUNG

It is my conviction that no child—none, at least, who is mentally sound—can avoid being occupied with sexual problems in the years before puberty.

—SIGMUND FREUD

A favorite teacher of mine once remarked, "Anyone without feelings or fantasies can safely be declared dead." Certainly, we humans typically have a high volume of images running around in our heads at any given time.

People have sexual feelings and fantasies for many reasons. A routine week in this society offers a great deal of sexual stimulation from films and TV, advertising, romance novels, and suggestive and revealing clothing. Most work, residential, and play environments also now mix the two sexes, frequently providing close physical contact.

Sexual anxieties are common primarily because of the cultural belief that there are correct ways to think, feel, and behave sexually. This belief implies, of course, that some ways are wrong or inadequate. The media tend to suggest that anyone who is sexually frustrated is, indeed, doing or feeling something wrong.

In fact, the media consciously encourage the feeling of sexual inadequacy in consumers. They then sell advertising to those whose products offer to alleviate that sense of inadequacy. Whether the product is alcohol, cars, cigarettes, underwear, or appliances, the promise is the same: use this and your anxiety will subside. Sociologist C. Wright Mills observed this dynamic twenty-five years ago, and it's truer today than ever before.

Three common misunderstandings about fantasies and feelings contribute to our desire for secrecy. The first is that we are all responsible for our fantasies and feelings; that if we are strong-willed, emotionally healthy, or highly spiritual, we will not create unusual or troubling mental images.

This simply is not true. As educator Sol Gordon says in his book, *The New You:* "Sexual thoughts, dreams, and daydreams are normal, no matter how far out. Behavior can be wrong, but ideas cannot be. Guilt is the energy for the repetition of unacceptable thoughts. The best way of keeping unacceptable thoughts under control is to accept them as normal."

Dr. Gordon gives an excellent example: A fifteen-year-old boy accidentally glimpses his sister showering. Momentarily excited, he feels evil and guilty for enjoying it. In reaction, he becomes hostile to his sister. As her naked image refuses to leave his mind, he becomes increasingly depressed. Had he understood that his excitement was normal, he could have allowed the image to fade by itself, along with the incident's importance.

According to the "you are responsible" concept, fantasies reflect the gap between who we are and who we should be. What an unfair, unnatural standard to hold people to! The belief that our fantasies indicate what we want, think we deserve, or feel is right is a grave moral error. It undermines the grand experience of taking responsibility for what we *can* control—our behavior.

The second common misunderstanding about fantasies and feelings is that they should always be taken at face value.

Now sometimes fantasies are definitely about what they seem to be about. When we conjure up images of an exotic stranger while masturbating, for example, pure sexual pleasure is generally just what we have in mind. Why do we deliberately fantasize? Because it's enjoyable.

There is, however, another side to fantasies and feelings.

You've certainly had the experience of snapping at family or friends when you're upset about work. And you've probably barked at a co-worker once or twice because you were aggravated about heavy traffic on the way to the office. These are ways of expressing feelings indirectly; that is, expressing one feeling rather than another one that lies underneath.

It's the same with fantasies. Instead of focusing on their content, we can often understand them better by examining their theme or tone. For in the unconscious (as reflected, say, in dreams and verbal slips), "Logic carries no weight," said Freud, "contradictory urges or ideas exist side by side." Adult considerations such as the literal truth are irrelevant to the unconscious. Its goal is merely to express emotional energy.

Look at the following examples of "troubling" sexual fantasies. Acting out these images would certainly cause problems and invite others' judgments. As fantasies, however, their themes express understandable and "normal" feelings that we all share. See if you agree with the suggested interpretations.

- *Fantasy:* A grown man daydreams about making love with the high school girls walking past his car as he waits at a red light.
  Expressing: The desire to be free and/or youthful again.
- *Fantasy:* A heterosexual college student imagines a homosexual orgy with his basketball teammates.
  Expressing: The desire to feel part of a special group, like a family (a wish that may particularly involve feeling close to father).
- *Fantasy:* A woman heightens the excitement and pleasure of lovemaking by imagining she's being raped.
  Expressing: After a week of powerlessness at work and at home, she seizes control by mentally directing intense, aggressive power.
- *Fantasy:* A devoted mother fantasizes about seducing each of the three workmen on her roof.
  Expressing: Concerns about still being sexy and attractive.
- *Fantasy:* A powerful executive masturbates to images of being tied up by a mean-looking woman dressed entirely in leather.
  Expressing: The wish to relinquish control or a too-heavy load of responsibility.
- *Fantasy:* A woman compulsively reads romance novels and imagines herself as the heroine, forced to submit to sex with a cruel stranger.
  Expressing: The wish to be valued so much that a man dishonors himself in order to pursue her.

Ultimately, most fantasies reflect either unconscious processes or the desire to satisfy basic emotional needs. This is why we can neither rationally evaluate them nor trust their content. And it is why they provide such valuable emotional release, and why they must not be subject to the same standards as behavior.

Make no mistake, however: you and I are unaware of such themes when we create our fantasies. Our only awareness in generating these images is that they enrich our sexual satisfaction.

A third misunderstanding concerns the sinfulness of allegedly "bad" thoughts. In therapy, people often express their fear of "bad" thoughts by describing a sense of vulnerability and powerlessness. Such feelings can be a dreadful reminder of adolescence, when new, unwanted sexual thoughts started appearing without warning.

Here's how Phyllis, a mother of three, describes her current experience: "Sometimes I feel like someone's taken over my head. I see a man in the market and I imagine going right over and asking to play with his penis.

"Of course I don't do it," she quickly adds, "but it disturbs me that the image comes to mind. It makes me feel that I've got to watch myself every second."

Many women enjoy creating such fantasies. "It makes marketing much less of a chore," says one. Still, many worry that the fantasizing isn't normal, and they wonder if they should stop.

"Or I'll be in bed with my husband," Phyllis continues, "and right in the middle of sex I'll think, 'What if I don't climax tonight? What if I never do again? It would just about ruin everything.' Fears like that—totally unrealistic, out of the blue—plus those supermarket feelings, make me worry that it's a mistake to just be myself. And all the while I'm smiling at my Harold, pretending that I'm calm, that there's no inner struggle."

Modern notions of morality focus far more on sexuality than on other aspects of daily life. As a result, institutions of authority claim the right to decide which expressions of sexuality are "normal." Most people typically judge the discrepancies between themselves and these norms as a problem with them, rather than with the norms. Predictably, this response is reinforced by the dominant culture. This dynamic is also discussed as a form of social pressure later in this chapter.

WHY WE DEVELOP SECRETS ABOUT FANTASIES AND FEELINGS

Various forms of the Secrecy Imperative explain much of the common drive toward keeping sexual fantasies and feelings secret. A look at childhood—specifically the structure of children's thought processes—will help us understand the feelings that typically surround adult fantasy life.

Starting in 1921, Swiss psychologist Jean Piaget documented the ways children think differently than adults. Concluding that the brain's mental capacities develop in an orderly, predictable fashion, he categorized the kinds of thinking characteristic of each stage of childhood.

Piaget saw children as actively creating and recreating their models of reality as they understood the world in increasingly complex terms. Paradoxically, part of that complexity includes understanding the true separateness and limited power of individual human beings.

Most relevant for our discussion are these points of Piaget's:

• Preschool children's notion of causality is "magical." They believe objects or events can act on each other simply because they are close to each other. For example, if you note how a stack of records fits nicely on a shelf next to the stereo, a child might easily respond, "Yes, the stereo moved over to make enough room."

• Six year olds cannot generally differentiate between the mental and the physical. Their notion of causality is still magical, but they now include their own thoughts as an important agent of cause. For example, if a child in a tantrum says he doesn't care if his frog dies, and the frog dies soon after, he could easily believe that he caused the frog's death.

• Preadolescents understand that their thoughts can't make objects move, but they still believe that their thoughts can be read by others or can influence them. For example, an eleven-year-old girl worries that she is the only one in her class who hasn't started menstruating. When another girl looks at her in the school locker room, the eleven-year-old could believe the girl knows what she's thinking.

• Adolescents understand the limitations of their thoughts, but they judge and then overgeneralize the moral meaning of their thoughts. For example, a white teen doesn't like another teen who happens to be black, from the very first impression. On reflection, the white boy might think, "That is prejudice, which is bad. I must be completely prejudiced, therefore completely bad."

• Children can develop a moral system only as quickly as their thinking apparatus develops. For example, three year olds can't really consider others' feelings because they cannot yet fully conceptualize the idea of "other." Another example is the heightened interest in justice and fair play that junior high school children express when they start developing the ability to think abstractly.

Thus, children learn to identify with and then separate from their thoughts in stages. "Realistic" and "logical" thought can only come in adulthood. And yet, all children strive mightily to make sense of the world around them. Doing so with the limited mental tools of childhood leads to some distorted, sadly destructive, results—like the Secrecy Imperative.

If one word sums up the world of the child, it is "magical." Not the magic of rabbits pulled from hats, but of various sources of power. One is the power of mere thought. Do you recall learning the following magic as a child?

- God knows all your thoughts (especially the "bad" ones)
- People can tell what you're thinking
- Bad thoughts lead to nightmares
- Bad thoughts can hurt people
- Bad thoughts cause pimples, deformities, and accidents
- Only bad people think bad thoughts
- Thinking about doing something bad is as bad as doing it

As this list of common childhood beliefs reveals, "bad thoughts" are considered dangerous. Youngsters, delightedly experimenting with their wonderful new abilities, cannot understand that the power of their thoughts is limited.

In addition, children *judge* their thoughts and feelings, using highly simplistic moral criteria. Young children can only grasp "good" and "bad." They literally cannot understand subtle moral distinctions, such as extenuating circumstances, competing interests, saving face, or sacrificing a small principle to secure a larger one.

Unfortunately, kids' distorted beliefs about their thoughts blur the difference between private mental activity and public behavior. This inhibits children's sense of owning their own minds, and makes imagination and creativity dangerous.

Since their ability to categorize is very primitive, children have trouble understanding what about a particular thought makes it "bad." The only plausible answer, for the child, is "everything," which includes the thinker as well.

It is only a short step, therefore, from "My thoughts are bad" to "*I* am bad." For example, almost all children wish to get rid of their infant siblings. But since this *wish* is "bad," they feel guilty for *being* "bad" unless their parents make it clear that such feelings are normal.

The problems of self-esteem, fear of intimacy, and lack of self-control resulting from children criticizing their own thoughts are well-documented. Many parents unwittingly encourage this distorted emotional development. Without thinking, they discount their child's feelings: "Oh, you don't hate your sister, nice girls don't hate anybody!" Or, "You don't wish your uncle were dead. God punishes little boys who wish such things."

Understandably, children are slow to give up the imagined power that comes with believing in the magic of their thoughts. Parents who suggest that the thinker of the criticized behavior deserves criticism only help maintain this childhood illusion. And since all children have predictable, uninvited thoughts (like incest and murder wishes), they become highly self-critical. The childhood conclusion that "I am bad" can be devastating.

The adult need for secrecy about thoughts and fantasies is an obvious consequence of childhood lessons about "bad thoughts" and the badness of those who think them.

During adolescence, children of each gender learn new reasons why sexual anxiety is inappropriate (and, therefore, to be kept secret). Boys learn that "real men" are sex experts, which makes any lack of confidence a betrayal of masculinity. Expecting this expertise, many women are turned off by any doubt or anxiety a man has about his adequacy.

Young women are, in fact, instructed to assume that men are sex experts. But they also learn that men's egos are fragile. Thus, if a woman is anxious about sex, it is an insult to her partner. The only other explanation is that she is not a "real woman"—that is, one who can relax and enjoy sex with a (presumed) "real man." So young men and women both learn that anxiety about sex is abnormal, a problem to be hidden. And another seed of secrecy is sown.

Children learn to hide their anxiety about sexuality as they watch their parents criticize each other's sex-role performance. Thus, they learn it is dangerous to share fears of inadequacy.

An engineer named Seymour told me a poignant story about this. "When I was about ten," he said, "my dad was laid off. At first it was neat having him around, but after a few months, the mood around the house became pretty grim.

One night I awoke to my parents discussing it. My dad said he was scared that he'd never find work again, and my mother blew up.

" 'I can handle you losing your job,' I remember her saying angrily. 'But you're scared, nervous about finding another one! What kind of man are you?' she yelled. 'What kind of a man gets scared?' My father just burst into tears, and my mother left the room.

"That rejection has stayed crystal-clear in my mind," says Seymour. "I learned right then that hiding and protecting yourself was a damn smart thing to do." Seymour's mother must have been so frightened that she couldn't tolerate anyone around her being anxious — especially the person who was supposed to be taking care of her.

Children also observe that when one adult tells another, "I'm upset," the reply is often, "Don't feel that way." Can't you just hear Cary Grant's response to all those distraught women, in film after film? "Now, now, stop crying. Don't be silly. There's nothing to be upset about." In real life, responses like that teach people to hide their feelings.

CULTURAL MESSAGES, SOCIAL PRESSURES

In addition to these dynamics, several kinds of social pressures encourage secrecy about our sexual feelings, anxieties, and fantasies.

America's mass media present a remarkably homogeneous set of images. Advertisements, magazine covers, and TV and film castings all offer the same predictable portrait of attractiveness in men and women. In this way, we are instructed on the kind of fantasy object that is most acceptable.

In fact, the media creates and presents the objects themselves. Current examples are Tom Selleck and Cybill Shepherd, who are revered as objects rather than as people. Our lust for them is impersonal precisely because they are public figures, completely unknown to us, and shared with millions of other adoring fans.

Our mates, to a degree, participate in our fantasies about such stars. Your partner knows about the fantasy object, generally agrees that the object represents perfection, and even that the object is more attractive than he or she is. No one needs to hide the fact that he finds Miss America attractive. What we tend to hide is our attraction to a neighbor or co-worker. That's precisely because we desire him or her as a person rather than as an object.

The media also encourages secrecy by invariably portraying heroes without sexual anxiety or other inconvenient feelings. Generations of men have modeled themselves after James Bond and John Wayne, characters who lack the normal anxiety, anger, disappointment, and frustration that interfere with the romantic relationships of real people.

Why aren't our relationships as perfect and thrilling as theirs? One reason is that James Bond isn't involved in intimacy. He's an object interacting with other objects. But real adults generally want this perfection *and* intimacy, which simply cannot be attained. In reaction, most of us deal with this discrepancy by hiding it. We develop the common belief that discussing anxiety or other feelings "breaks the mood" or creates distance.

Another social pressure encouraging secrecy is the cultural belief that 1) certain thoughts are "bad;" and 2) thinking "bad" thoughts is as bad as doing bad things.

We have already suggested, at length, that there are no "bad thoughts," only "bad" (that is, destructive) behaviors. Some religious views, unfortunately, make "bad thoughts" an absolute cornerstone of belief. According to the 1976 *New Catholic Encyclopedia* "The act of thinking can be good or evil. . . . The attention of Catholic moralists has centered chiefly upon evil rather than upon good thoughts. Morality is primarily a matter of the heart; [this is recalled in the] Pauline theme of . . . the primacy of attitude over acts."

This view truly stands human experience on its head. Aren't most of us concerned first with how someone treats us, and only second with what thoughts they have? Yet, this religious doctrine presumes to judge private thoughts, even to the exclusion of our righteous deeds.

This insidious doctrine goes even further. Look at how serious a moral crime it is to enjoy or even tolerate "sinful" fantasies or feelings: "The quality of the sin is the same as that of the corresponding exterior act; for example, an actual murder." In simple language: if doing something is evil, thinking about doing it without immediate moral judgment is *just as evil.*

No one who believes this doctrine would dare admit to a friend or loved one that he had done the spiritual equivalent of rape, incest, infidelity, group sex, or exposing himself. Realistically, people conceal such thoughts, condemning themselves as "sick."

HOW WE KEEP SECRETS

The secrets we have about our fantasies or anxieties are often hidden from ourselves as well as from others. We don't do this deliberately. Rather, we do it through unconscious maneuvers designed to keep us unaware of painful feelings. Freud called these maneuvers "defense mechanisms," mental activities meant to "defend" us from the pain of feeling guilty or evil for having unacceptable thoughts.

Let's look at how this is done.

The first defense is called *projection.* This is when you unconsciously attribute a feeling that you can't accept as your own to another person. People who project a lot get involved in needless conflict, as they respond to insults, threats, challenges, seductions, and other emotional events that aren't really there, or aren't about them.

One of the predictable results of projection is emotional

distance. This was the problem of a forty-year-old man I counseled.

Julio was a county employee who married his college sweetheart, Lupe, the day after they graduated. Lupe insisted he see me because of his jealous rages. "He swears I'm having affairs," she said in exasperation, "which is crazy. He has no evidence, and I have no interest in other men. He says he knows that I love him. What's wrong with the guy?"

Julio turned out to be a warm, articulate man who was also confused by the situation. While acknowledging that he didn't have any real evidence of Lupe's cheating, he said that strong feelings periodically came over him without warning. At those times he would become nasty and difficult to live with.

How did a rational, intelligent man handle these irrational episodes? "I suppose you'd say that it's crazy to accuse her of cheating that way," he said blandly, "but maybe it isn't. After all, almost everyone has affairs, you know. Everyone but me."

It was an odd thing to say, so I asked Julio why he didn't have affairs. "I'm not that type," he said. "You know— selfish, irresponsible. Like my dad." He dropped the clue rather casually. Julio's father, apparently, had been the talk of their small Oregon town, sleeping with widows, teenagers, and hitchhikers with equal abandon. It had destroyed their home life. "Worst of all," Julio later recalled bitterly, "the other kids teased me about it."

No wonder Julio was eager to dissociate himself from his destructive father. Unconsciously fearing his vulnerability to Lupe's behavior, he tried to control it with preemptive strikes. His accusations were, unconsciously, meant to prevent her from ruining his life, or catch her trying to.

But I believed there was more. Did Julio ever daydream about having an affair of his own? "I told you," he said impatiently, "I've never had an affair. I never would." Could Julio differentiate between fantasy and behavior? I questioned him about daydreams once more, and received the same curt answer.

Taking a calculated risk, I pressed on. "Julio, most men think about having affairs, even if they never have them. Are you—"

"That's being unfaithful," he interrupted. "I wouldn't do that."

We were getting closer; I pushed again. "So when you see a beautiful woman on the street, or in a movie, do you—"

"I put it out of my mind!" he yelled. "I'm not going to let it control me. I won't let anyone know I think these things." He was shaking.

The room echoed with Julio's powerful emotions. Although his thoughts were normal, he found them unacceptable. It was understandable, given his background. His dad's affairs had hurt the entire family, and Julio was determined that he wasn't going to do the same.

So what could he do with his "dangerous" sexual thoughts about other people? Project them onto Lupe, and attempt to control them from a safer distance. Ironically, his unpredictable attacks created exactly the same isolation and sadness that he was trying so desperately to avoid. Julio had a secret: he thought about sex with other women. If he could only accept the normalcy of these thoughts, he would have many more options for dealing with them. That became the focus of our work together.

The following are other defense mechanisms we use to keep secrets from ourselves.

Repression is a common way of hiding the truth from ourselves, often with alcohol. Chemicals are this culture's accepted medium for avoiding painful facts and feelings. They are also used to create and maintain sexual secrets. Some men never know they feel threatened by powerful women because they only go out (or make love) after they've had a joint or several drinks.

Blame is another form of self-deception. We use blame when it's difficult to admit what we want, or when we feel more comfortable believing that others control our choices. Teenagers and others who have trouble taking responsibility for themselves often use this defense.

One woman I used to work with would become extremely aroused fantasizing about her husband with another woman (which is fairly common). She said she wanted to use the fantasy in their lovemaking, but felt that she couldn't because he'd never stop talking about it. She blamed him for preventing her from doing what she wanted, but couldn't bring herself to do.

Reaction formation involves doing the opposite of what you'd unconsciously like to do, but feel you must not. Some people want to ban nude beaches, for example, to prove to themselves that they don't really want to look at naked people—which they do. In this way they keep their secret from themselves, if not from cynical observers. The rest of us pay for their blissful self-ignorance with restrictions on our civil liberties.

Simple *deception* is a common way to hide secrets about sex-related fear or anxiety. A nurse named Gwen, for example, came to see me about her difficulty climaxing. What made it a real problem lately, she said, was her increased sex drive since having a hysterectomy.

Gwen was a bit older than many of the men in her department, and she felt she had to compete with younger women. She believed that they all had an easy time climaxing (not true), which would make her anxiety laughable to a new partner. On top of everything else, Gwen also believed her anxiety would offend a man, who would feel it reflected a lack of trust in his lovemaking ability.

To handle her anxiety, Gwen hid it, and used cocaine before making love with anyone. This helped her relax and focus on the pleasure. Unfortunately, the coke was giving her a hangover, was sometimes difficult to hide, and was unhealthy. Although Gwen was not addicted, she hesitated to stop because she had no other way of handling her anxiety.

Committed to secrecy about her feelings, Gwen was really stuck. Above all, she needed to accept her anxiety as "normal," which would give her the choice of sharing it or concealing it. Either way, she would feel better about herself.

Denial is a familiar childhood way of attempting to keep a secret. It reflects the magical belief that if I say it isn't so, it isn't so. Denial is a very primitive, or childish, defense.

You've probably had the experience, during sex, of sensing that your partner was worried, nervous, or distracted. "What's the matter?" you gently inquire. "Nothing," you're told, or "Just a lot on my mind. Forget it."

This is the way we teach our partners (especially women) to discount their senses and to go ahead with sex under negative conditions. The anxious partner also learns one more time that feeling isolated is the normal context of sexuality.

Then there's the other kind of denial, aimed toward limiting a partner's knowledge rather than our own. Lenny Bruce used to tell a story about the way some men would deny sexual feelings or behavior despite the most blatant evidence to the contrary:

A woman's suspected her husband's infidelity for a long time, but hasn't had any proof. One day she comes home early and finds him in bed with another woman. "It's not what you think," he says to her calmly. "You miserable liar," she shouts. "Now, dear, it's not what it looks like," he suggests genially. "You can't be trusted one bit," she cries. "Honey," the man soothes, "who are you going to believe— your lying eyes, or your loving husband?"

FANTASIES

According to Masters and Johnson, "Sexual fantasies begin in childhood and serve important functions in our lives, such as combating boredom, providing or enhancing excitement, releasing inner tensions, and permitting safe, imaginary rehearsals of untried behavior." They continue into adulthood, serving these and other purposes.

The range of common sexual fantasies is enormous. As sexologist Dr. Charles Moser says, "No one can imagine the entire range of normal sexual fantasies, no matter how way-out his own fantasies are." And yet, secrecy prevents people from knowing how common their own fantasies are.

This is particularly true of women, who have never had *Playboy*-type magazines. This isolation led Nancy Friday and Lonnie Barbach to write their books of women's erotica. The goal was "To let women know about others' sexy thoughts and feelings," says Barbach, "and to give permission for these fantasies."

Secrecy about fantasies has the same isolating, demeaning effects as other sexual secrets. Of course, not every fantasy is best revealed—lust for your brother-in-law may be better kept secret—but, as we have said all along, more important than revealing your secrets is accepting them as normal. Two related stories make this point.

When Jon called me to set up our first appointment, he said he was worried about his mental health. On the day of our first session, a virtual twin of Alan Alda walked in. He had a warm and gentle manner. After some pleasant preliminaries, he told me about his loneliness.

"It's simple," he said. "When I masturbate I think of doing things that worry me. Like I'm forcing women to have oral sex with me, or I'm seducing young girls. I even imagine getting my brother's wife drunk and half raping her," he said ruefully.

"I'd never do these things. So why do I think them? Why do they make my orgasms so fabulous? I feel very alone," Jon continued. "Who can I tell about this? Nobody. Nobody I ever want to see again, that's for sure."

Poor Jon. He didn't understand that such fantasies are

very common. Our conversation led me to believe that he had no interest in being violent or manipulative, and I told him that I found his fantasies acceptable. It was a powerful experience for him, being fully accepted after revealing his darkest secret. Our therapy progressed quickly. I don't think he ever told anyone else about his fantasies, but he did begin to accept himself. That was what he needed the most.

Here's another view of the same story; call it the other side of the coin, if you wish.

A well-known author I'll call Cindy came to see me. "Sex is fine, better than fine," she started, "except for one thing. I have this totally unacceptable fantasy. It's big black men holding me down, taking turns screwing me. In the fantasy I have one giant orgasm after another, which triggers the real thing."

And that was totally unacceptable? "Yes," she answered emphatically. "It's just not me, that powerless crap. You know where I am politically." Indeed, I was very familiar with her sophisticated feminist work. "I feel guilty and very embarrassed about these fantasies," she continued. "But I love them. They make my orgasms incredibly hot, whether I'm alone or with a man."

Cindy felt she couldn't share her distress, not with her lovers and certainly not with her friends or feminist comrades. Her embarrassment was additional proof, she reasoned, that the fantasies were bad. "Or maybe I'm not the committed feminist I thought I was," she said. "That would kill me."

Neither Cindy nor Jon understood the nature of fantasy, nor the concept that thinking about a situation does not mean desiring it. Why then did they fantasize behavior that they had no interest in carrying through?

As therapist Dr. Jack Morin, author of the forthcoming *Cornerstones of Eroticism,* says, "Almost everyone fantasizes. And in order to intensify our sexual response, we produce fantasies in which we overcome some psychological distance.

That distance can involve, for example, taboos or physical danger, both very common fantasy themes." That certainly describes both Cindy's and Jon's fantasies. Both scenarios allow response to situations that are not "supposed" to be enjoyed. That element alone creates tremendous arousal.

The troubling fantasies that people hide range from the exotic to the homespun. After a lecture I gave in Pittsburgh, a woman approached me. "I love my husband, Donn, very much," she said. "But sometimes I think about Robert Redford when I make love with him. It troubles me." She seemed to need reassurance very much.

"Don't you think Donn would agree," I asked, "that fantasizing about Robert Redford while making love with your husband is preferable to thinking of your husband while making love to Robert Redford?"

She thought about it and began to smile. "I guess it's like you said in your talk," she mused. "If it works for me, that defines what's normal for me, right?"

I smiled as broadly as she did. "Right," I said, with great satisfaction.

ANXIETY—A VERY SPECIAL FEELING

Human beings experience a remarkable range of feelings, and anxiety is one of the most common and unpleasant. Mental health professionals unanimously agree that anxiety plays a destructive role in sexual functioning.

Bernie Zilbergeld says in *Male Sexuality* that sexual messages from the brain to the genitals "must be clearly sent and received. If the nervous system is obstructed, the messages to the [genitals] don't get through properly. The most common obstructor during sex is nervous tension or anxiety. [It] throws the whole nervous system into a tizzy, obstructing the transmission of sexual messages."

What's worse than feeling anxious? The certainty that

you must keep the anxiety secret. Here is a description of just such a situation.

A woman named Denise was sent to me by her company's personnel counselor because of complaints that she wasn't self-directed enough. I quickly saw that Denise wanted to please everyone, and that she felt incapable of doing so.

As our work together progressed, Denise realized that she wanted more supervision on the job, along with more support and encouragement. It took a while, but eventually she was able to ask for these changes, and her performance improved almost immediately. At that point she asked if we could talk about her marriage, especially about sex.

"I worry a lot," she said simply. "Am I really satisfying James? Does he like my body? What if he's holding back because of me? How do you know if you're good in bed?" She didn't dare tell James, but Denise had a sexual secret: she was anxious about her adequacy.

It was similar to her work issue. She needed to feel more connected to those around her. But she wasn't sure she deserved it, and wasn't comfortable asking for it.

Where had she gotten the idea that she wasn't sexually adequate? "Well," she started, "I was taught that you're either a nice girl or a sexy one, right? Of course, I like to think I'm one of the nice girls. Besides, the sexy ones are young and slim. These thighs will never see twenty-five again," she chuckled sadly.

As I listened, I noted Denise's assumptions: that she had to choose between being nice and sexy, that "of course" she'd choose the former, and that there was only one way to define sexy. Rather than abruptly confront her about these myths, I encouraged her to continue. I knew we'd return to these ideas eventually.

Continuing, Denise revealed that a series of emotionally abusive "normal" boyfriends were also part of the picture. "My college boyfriend? He called himself 'a man's man' and said I was lucky that he was my first. Afterward he told me I was lucky that he was so patient. He made it clear that I wasn't, and would never be, really sexy."

Nice guy, I thought to myself. *He* should pay for the therapy. Because, now that Denise is married, she's unsure of her sexual attractiveness. Worse still, she can't share her concerns with her husband. "He'd take it personally," she said, believing that that was a good enough reason to isolate herself. "It's better he not know what's wrong."

In reality, Denise's silence reflects *her* judgment about her insecurity, not her husband's. She simply believes it's wrong to feel that way, and that no man should be asked to deal with it. Denise is hypersensitive to anything that looks like a demand, fearing she'll be abandoned if she asks for anything.

Secrecy about performance anxiety takes many forms. Because of early lessons about "manliness," this tends to be a particularly problematic experience for men.

The subject reminds me of Lawrence, a big, likable guy who was a brakeman on a San Francisco cable car. He enjoyed his work, especially the chance to meet so many people. His friendliness made it easy to start relationships, both with tourists and locals.

"I'm here to talk about dating," he began our first session. "Everything goes fine, until it's clear that the woman is interested in sex. Then something happens. We get into a fight, I decide it wasn't such a good idea, one of us loses interest, whatever. I'm really mystified," he said. "And horny."

I wondered why a man who enjoyed making contact with people kept arranging not to have sex. While talking about what he liked and disliked about lovemaking, Lawrence mentioned his concern about "doing it right." He said he wanted to be "the best lover in the world," but he sometimes worried that he wasn't.

Did he share this anxiety with his lovers? "No," he said,

"of course not." And why not? He looked at me, somewhat confused. "No one does, do they? I mean, I wouldn't think of telling a woman I was concerned about my performance."

When I again asked Lawrence why not, he said he didn't have a specific reason. "It's something I've always taken for granted." Then I ran down some common feelings of people who feel obliged to hide their anxiety about sex. Was it any of these?

- You'll think I'm silly
- You'll leave me
- I don't know how you'll respond
- I don't feel close enough to you for such intimate sharing
- It will make my anxiety worse

No, it wasn't any of these, Lawrence said, growing more restless by the minute. "I've had enough questions," he boomed. "I hate feeling this way. It's totally uncool to worry about your damn hard-on . . . the hell with sex!" The room was silent.

I observed the outburst calmly, without replying. Clearly, Lawrence had sexual anxiety, and, just as clearly, he was ashamed of it. Therefore he tried to hide it. And the way he hid it was by unconsciously aborting potential sexual inter-actions. That allowed him to avoid the painful possibility of not performing perfectly.

"You know," I finally said, "you're not the first person to raise his voice in this room." Lawrence looked at me quiz-zically. "In fact, everyone with your sexual concern gets up-set one way or another. I guess I'm more used to it than you are." Lawrence wasn't sure how to take this, so I continued.

"People don't need good reasons to be concerned about their sexual performance," I said. "Look around you. Bill-boards, movies, and magazines can scare someone enough to swear off sex altogether. And," I added, "make you think you're the only one who feels that way."

As Lawrence slowly smiled, I knew I'd gotten through to him. "You're saying it's normal to be nervous," he said. "I bet you're even going to say that it's normal to try and hide it." I simply nodded, letting him enjoy the insight. It only took a few more sessions to help Lawrence accept his feelings. Once he did, his need to avoid sex decreased dramatically. We were able to terminate therapy soon after.

A second type of anxiety involves privacy, specifically the concern that a partner will reveal the relationship to others. Privacy is typically an issue when the relationship involves the "outside world" through social status or economic concerns. Examples include:

- A man having an extramarital affair with a woman who doesn't know that he's married
- An executive woman seeing a blue-collar worker
- A woman with a well-cultivated reputation as a virgin
- A middle-aged professor dating a college student
- A shy woman who does not want to be known as someone with a very high sex drive
- A man who knows his partner is sexually dissatisfied

The Secrecy Imperative explains why people typically hide privacy anxieties. They believe they shouldn't have such feelings, and assume that their partners would judge them if they knew the truth.

In some cases, these concerns are based on reality. The blue-collar worker, for example, might feel angry that his uptown friend does not want anyone to know they are lovers. Some partners even end relationships once they discover why privacy is desired. This often happens with extramarital affairs in which the unmarried partner has been deceived.

But in many cases our partners understand our need for privacy. Even when they don't, they often choose to respect it anyway.

People give many other reasons for keeping their anxiety secret:

- I'm not supposed to care about keeping our relationship private
- I don't want to acknowledge that you have power over me
- I feel embarrassed about being anxious
- I don't want to appear foolish
- I'm afraid you'll feel that I don't trust you

Such concepts can be traced back to the Secrecy Imperative. They are nearly always projections of our own feelings and self-criticism onto those close to us.

The woman with the virginal reputation, for example, knows she is deceiving people. She feels guilty about it, and projects her guilt onto her lover, believing *he* couldn't handle her anxiety about losing her valued reputation.

Two ironies about "anxiety secrecy" are worth noting here. First, many people believe that talking about anxiety makes it worse. Such intimate talk, they say, is just "feeling sorry for yourself." But talking about anxiety is a great way to get close to someone.

Second, keeping your anxiety secret from your lover removes the most effective anti-anxiety tool, which is talking about the feelings. There may be costs to doing so—there is the risk of rejection—but that does not negate the point. Talking about anxiety almost invariably reduces it. Secrecy makes that talk impossible.

Talking about anxiety makes intimacy possible. Some people feel that that's worth just about any risk.

OTHER FEELINGS

Fear and anger are two other feelings often associated with sex. Many feel obligated to keep these secret because of social pressure. "You're not supposed to have those feelings about sex," states one client angrily. "And if you do, they are not supposed to affect your behavior."

Bernie Zilbergeld writes in *Male Sexuality*, "There is a common belief that the second we get involved in a sexual situation, we should be able to put our feelings aside. I have worked with many men, for example, who demand that they be able to get erections even with women they don't like. To me, that's one way to create sexual problems."

Many clients need educating about this exact point. One of the nicer people I have worked with is a supermarket checker named Norma, whose complaint was lack of orgasm. A medical review showed no physiological problems. "I don't expect to climax every time I make love," she said, "but I would like to have them much more often."

A few weeks later, Norma came to our session with her boyfriend, Mark, a professional baseball player. They don't look that big on TV, but this guy just about filled up the waiting room.

I don't recall exactly how it came up, but we were soon talking about "perfect" sex. "It would be better for me," said Norma quietly, "if you were smaller." Mark was genuinely surprised: "I thought you loved my body!" "I do," Norma continued, "but it's also, umm, overwhelming. You don't know how scary you can be." Surprised herself to hear the words, she looked away.

Hurt, Mark lashed out. "I don't understand. I try to be a good lover, don't I? I'm usually gentle. What are you so afraid of? Why are you so hung up on me saying I love you?"

"Because sex is scary, period," Norma replied. "If *you* were on your back naked, and had someone twice your size bouncing around on top of you *and* had part of their body inside yours, you might be nervous too," she said. "I bet you'd want to hear 'I love you' a lot."

The secret was out: Norma wanted more *attention* during sex. All three of us now understood her lack of orgasms, which wasn't so odd after all. I suggested that she and Mark discuss specific ways they could make sex more *personal*. "Hey, I wouldn't mind some more of that myself," Mark said with a laugh. They agreed to work on it together at home.

Another woman who had difficulty climaxing was Tracy, a newlywed. "I don't understand it," she said at our first session. "The sex is great. Herb is a fabulous lover. So why is it getting harder and harder for me to come?"

I asked about her new marriage. It was terrific, Tracy exclaimed. She loved "our house, our dog, his parents, our parties, my new job. . . ."

Notice what's missing? What about their relationship? That, it turned out, wasn't quite perfect. "I guess we argue a lot," admitted Tracy. "And you know men. When Herb doesn't get his way, he loses his temper. Sometimes he leaves the house."

Every marriage, of course, has conflict, but partners need to know they can express themselves without being punished. Tracy knew just the opposite: that telling the truth about her needs and feelings would result in being attacked or abandoned. And so, very often, she didn't.

How did she feel about that? "Oh, okay. Maybe a little irritated," she said. I looked at her and said nothing. "Okay, more than a little," she offered. "Okay, I'm angry, so what? That doesn't solve anything, does it?" Tears started to form in her eyes. "Besides, that shouldn't stop me from climaxing."

Herb didn't really know the extent of her anger, did he? "No," Tracy sniffed. "He'd yell or call me names. Probably leave for the evening. I'm better off this way," she said.

"Not as far as sex goes," I said gently. Her genitals were saying what the rest of her couldn't: "I'm angry. I feel abandoned. It isn't safe to be me here."

Orgasms require letting go. Tracy couldn't climax easily because the marriage in general had no room for her to let go and be herself. The fact that she couldn't discuss her feelings with Herb illustrated that perfectly.

Tracy left my office unsure of what she'd do. She wanted to keep her feelings secret a while longer, hoping a new position or a weekend away would improve their sex life. I doubted it. When the brain and genitals disagree, the genitals always win. Tracy's vulva would keep expressing the outrage that the rest of her felt.

The story did end happily, although it took a while. About six months later, Tracy returned to therapy, this time with her husband. They had finally reached the point where they were willing to do *anything* to make sex better. Their marital therapy was painful at times, but it was successful. Not only did sex become rewarding, they learned how to talk to each other about many other things as well.

Feelings and thoughts are the building blocks of human relationships. Judging them "incorrect," or hiding them, strikes at the heart of our dignity and self-esteem. How do people feel when they hide sexual thoughts and feelings? Lonely, isolated, angry, inadequate, phony, afraid of discovery, and prone to anxiety.

We are a society with rigid cultural standards about "proper" feelings and thoughts. These standards make secrecy about feelings and fantasies especially common—and destructive.

Freeing ourselves from the compulsive need to be proper is an important part of growing up. At the same time, establishing reasonable limits for ourselves is also important. Finding a healthy balance between the two is one of the great challenges of adulthood.

6

THE
PAST

I think it all started when my mother caught me masturbating and had me registered as a sex offender.

—WOODY ALLEN

As you know, the focus of this book is not *revealing* your sexuality, but *owning* it. I would like to help you decide that regardless of your judgments (or those of others, real or imagined), you are okay. Some people call this forgiving yourself. Others say it involves reclaiming your past.

What would you be forgiving? Past choices and experiences that you might arrange differently if given the chance today. A friend of mine, for example, did not tell her fiancé she was sterile until after they were engaged. She'd tell him sooner if she could do it all over again, but she recognizes today that at the time, she was doing the best she could.

And what would you be reclaiming? The reality that your past behavior is a part of you. A great example occurred

in 1972 when a group of women, organized by Gloria Stei-
nem, signed a full-page ad in *The New York Times* demanding the legalization of abortion and affirming that they had
all had illegal abortions in the past.

The chance to make peace with yourself is the first important reason to discuss your secret-keeping about the past.
As you'll see in this chapter, reclaiming the past

- allows us to forgive others
- redistributes power in our relationships
- frees the future from imagined constraints

How does reclaiming the past do these things? First, by
allowing us to stop hiding. We can still regret something
we've done, but accepting and moving beyond it allows us
to contact others with our full selves. As we have seen
throughout this book, such contact is an important key to
relationship and life satisfaction.

Second, reclaiming the past interrupts the common life
script of "Because of what I did in the past, I don't get (nor
do I deserve) good things." Such a script is responsible for
chronic self-destructive patterns such as relationships with al-
coholics; failing to advance in jobs, school, or volunteer or-
ganizations; or an inability to permanently lose weight or quit
smoking cigarettes.

Owning your past lets you see yourself as a good person
who made particular choices, one who still deserves good
things regardless of the outcome of those choices. It also gives
you the freedom to determine your own life, instead of feeling
that it is predetermined by the past.

This "get on with it" attitude is the opposite of "I'll never
escape the fact that I was born on the wrong side of the tracks,"
or "I was a bad girl back then and I'll be paying for it the
rest of my life."

And owning your past, finally, lets you reintegrate lost
parts of yourself. Survival, as a child, often seems to require

giving up our intuition, openness, and willingness to experiment. But those qualities are part of us. Welcoming them back into your psyche is like welcoming home a friend you didn't realize you missed so badly.

After you have forgiven yourself, you have the choice of revealing or maintaining sexual secrets about your past. Part III will help you decide how to handle your secrets.

FEELINGS ABOUT THE PAST

During a typical week, I meet many people with strong feelings about their sexual past. Most of them feel alone, doubting that anyone could understand their situation or be in a similar one. How do we feel about the past? People tell me

- "It feels like it happened to someone else."
- "I was foolish," or "I made mistakes."
- "If I'm not careful it will sneak up and get me."

Think about how you feel about your own past. Are you aware of any of these common feelings?

- I should have known better
- I asked for trouble
- I don't deserve good things
- I judge my past behavior by my present wisdom and needs
- I should be judged more harshly than others
- I deserve punishment for being victimized
- Certain things should not be forgiven
- Forgiveness means approval
- The past has no logic of its own
- My past is worse than others'
- No one would understand how it was

Can you see how such feelings would distort your evaluation of your past and of others' reactions to it? These feelings are intimately connected to the four principal reasons people keep their past secret:

1. Inaccurate views of the past
2. The pursuit of other goals
3. Relationship dynamics
4. Cultural concepts

Let's examine each one in turn.

The Secrecy Imperative distorts our view of the past. This is particularly true regarding our assumptions about

- The seriousness of what we've done
- The consequences of what we've done
- How others will react to what we've done
- How we should be judged for what we've done

Take Monica, a thirty-five-year-old, straight-as-an-arrow accountant. She never had casual flings; in fact, when an irritating vaginal sore was diagnosed as herpes several years ago, she was in the middle of a period of abstinence. Monica was shocked and repulsed.

"I don't even know who I got it from," she cried. "How's that for prim and proper?" (The virus can lie dormant for years before the first outbreak.) "I feel dirty and guilty," she continued angrily. "That's why I don't tell anyone about it." She abstains when she's infectious, which is about twice a year.

Unfortunately, Monica has had a string of unsatisfying relationships since her first outbreak. She doesn't believe that a "nice guy" would be interested in "damaged goods," and so she unconsciously avoids nice guys. As "damaged goods," she doesn't feel she deserves any better than the dependent, selfish guys who have been ripping her off for five years. She's paying for her "dreadful" past, unnecessarily.

Given her frustration with the way things worked out,

what should Monica have done differently? Should she have been celibate? More "careful"? (She *was* careful, but even nice, clean people get herpes.) In any event, Monica has made her decisions. Although she may regret some of them (hindsight is, after all, 20/20), she certainly doesn't deserve punishment.

Unfortunately, Monica cannot see that. Her judgment is clouded by a punitive Secrecy Imperative, distorting her view of her behavior's consequences. Her inner voice says, "If it's about me and my sexuality, it must be bad." Monica's punitive side uses the herpes as proof. Her self-criticism is particularly ironic when compared with the loving support she'd give a friend in the same circumstances.

Once again, the Secrecy Imperative can be seen distorting our perceptions about the way we manifest our sexuality. It makes us harsh critics—unfair prosecutors rather than fair magistrates.

So how can you establish a balanced perspective about your past?

• Become aware of judging yourself. Instead of taking your critical voice for granted, recognize it as an unwanted mental intrusion. Whenever Monica thinks of herself as "damaged goods," she must remind herself, "No, I am not. I simply have a common virus which affects my life very little."

• Become absolutely clear that you can be okay regardless of your past decisions. Monica at some point chose to have unprotected sex. As a person, Monica is far bigger than this or any other decision she has made. Having resumed using condoms, she has no reason to keep castigating herself.

• Create new, explicit, gentle criteria with which to appraise yourself. For example, "Am I learning from past outcomes?" "Am I dealing with the sources of distortion and negativity?" "Am I supporting myself and others' positivity?"

• Stroke yourself when you meet those criteria. Be open to evidence that you are growing as a self-loving person, and then celebrate it! Buy yourself a small treat. Take a friend to lunch. Pay to have your car washed.

• Become aware of people or situations by which you are predictably attacked, and take positive steps to cope with or eliminate those relationships. If a seven-day family visit always involves five days of criticism and domination, make it a three-day visit instead, or even two separate one-day visits.

A second reason why people keep the past secret is that they use secrecy to pursue various unconscious goals. For some, the past contains more excitement than shame. One of my Asian clients, for example, frequently reminisces about the several black men she covertly had sex with before marrying her husband. This kind of secrecy is often a form of nostalgia. It offers a way to keep alive a past in which we felt more attractive, or full of potential, or able to enjoy life with less responsibility.

Although we may convince ourselves that this secrecy is crucial, it may primarily express our commitment to hold on to the past. While grieving for our losses is difficult, the payoff is full commitment to the present.

Another use of secrecy about the past is the chance to play out destructive personality scripts. Take people who grow up in abusive homes, like Natalie. Very early, Natalie developed the belief that men are no good and that trusting them is a mistake. As an adult, she unconsciously pursues this conviction in every relationship.

One of the ways she does so is by making closeness difficult by hiding her past. In addition to her abusive background, she withholds anything about herself that could facilitate intimacy. Another client hides the fact that she wrote erotic poetry in college. Another conceals the story of her two-year engagement to a marine killed in Vietnam. Each of these women can "prove" how hard it is to be close to men.

Playing out such a script also encourages a partner's secrecy. Natalie and people like her often feel insecure when given information about their partner's past. "I knew I shouldn't have trusted you," she said after a boyfriend revealed he had once been caught exposing himself in public. "You're probably dying to do it again," she said bitterly. Such reactions often bring about the very behavior that is feared. Once more, Natalie would get to be right.

A third reason for secrecy is that certain relationship dynamics exploit the past. Some people use a partner's past to control the relationship they're in. An educated woman may continually remind her less educated husband: "You're good with your hands, dear, but please leave the thinking to me." Another tactic is to comment on a mate's personal history in public. One jealous man, for example, loudly mentions his wife's background as a topless dancer whenever they're at a party where she gets any male attention.

This is a subtle form of manipulation that makes a partner feel powerless and vulnerable. Each of us has the right to decide what parts of our past are beyond routine comment via teasing, questions, or arguments.

If you can't seem to get a partner to respect your decisions about your past, assume that some kind of power play is going on and address it on that level: "Sam, I've said that your continual mention of my affair during my first marriage is very uncomfortable for me, yet you persist. What could you be getting out of it that is more important to you than my discomfort?"

Sam's unwanted teasing makes his wife regret disclosing her affair. Secrecy is the natural recourse of people who have their past used against them.

The anticipation of criticism also encourages secrecy. When a loved one says, "We all know that group sex is bad," we typically translate that to mean "Don't reveal that you've had group sex."

So, you can understand the importance of the question: Who gets to decide what parts of your past are eligible for criticism? Is it your decision, which your partner agrees to? Or does someone else (spouse, parent, or even child) impose his or her decision on you? I believe it should be *your decision alone,* and I encourage you to reject others' attempts to impose their values on you.

Why? Because we don't really accept values that others impose on us. At most, we tolerate them, but such tolerance is short-lived. Eventually, we grow resentful about not having the space we need to be ourselves. We might even deliberately violate the imposed values to assert our independence.

If a couple has seriously contrasting values, professional help is needed in order for them to live harmoniously. Unresolved, serious value conflicts often breed mistrust, hostility, and secrecy.

When one person in a relationship imposes his or her sexual values on another, two basic questions are raised:

1. Why is Partner One doing that to Partner Two?
2. Why is Partner Two allowing Partner One to do it?

Why is one partner doing that to the other? Imposing values on someone can be a way of defining that person's past. Being bullied into believing that you were corrupted in college by some homosexuals, for example, and dropping your belief that you were consciously experimenting, changes the meaning of your previous relationships, choices, and identity.

Redefining a partner's past is a means of controlling him or her. A partner might want to do that as a selfish, unfair way of handling any of these common feelings:

- "I am uncomfortable with your definition of your past."
- "I feel left out of your past. I don't want it to be complete or satisfactory without me."
- "I'm afraid I can't stop you from repeating that in the future."

The most common situation of controlling-by-imposing-values is a man attempting to redefine the sexually active past of a new mate. Although most men want their partners to be interested in sex with them, many are uncomfortable with the idea of free-floating female sexuality. Their feeling could be described as, "I want a woman's sexual interest to lie dormant, except when directed at me personally."

This, of course, is not always the reality, particularly as more and more women seize their own power and independence. Still, some men will "explain" a woman's sexual history by suggesting that she was "going through a phase," "rebelling," "experimenting," or even that she was "exploited." All of which is to say that her behavior was unacceptable. Which leads women to keep it secret.

Back to question 2: Why would one partner allow the other to impose outside sexual values on him/her?

People give away the power to define their sexual past for several reasons. The Secrecy Imperative pushes us in that direction. We think, "If it's my sexuality, it's suspect. If you say that someone like me is bad, you're probably right."

Here's a slightly different version of this dynamic: "You think someone like me is immoral. I'm not positive, but you may be right. And if I disagree with you, you'll feel certain that I'm immoral, and you may be even more right. So to play it safe, I'll let you decide what kind of past is appropriate, and I'll hide anything that doesn't fit that standard."

Believing the other person knows better is a common reason for relinquishing power. This is illustrated in the following two-part story. I'll present it in chronological order, although it wasn't given to me in such a convenient form.

Between her first and second marriages, a realtor named Janice went to Lake Tahoe for a long weekend with a girlfriend. They had a great time and became very close, and on their last night there they made love. "I had wondered what it would be like," said Janice, "and the moment, somehow, was perfect."

Even though they both enjoyed it, they had no interest in pursuing that part of their relationship. They are still friends. In fact, Pam was maid of honor at Janice's second wedding.

A few years after Janice married her second husband, Paul, they saw a film that featured an ambiguous female friendship. Although Janice thought the movie fun, Paul went on for days about "perverted lesbians." He claimed that "real" women weren't attracted to each other, and that those who are were dangerous to their kids. "And I should know," huffed Paul. "Who knows women better than a man who's been around?"

The marathon monologue disturbed Janice. She had never told Paul about the weekend with Pam; it was her warm, offbeat, private little memory. Now she was torn. Paul seemed so sure about this. And was Janice really dangerous to their one year old?

Janice's warm memory was now a frightening secret. The more anxious she became, the harder it was to put it out of her mind. She began to obsess about the incident and its meaning, and periodically became depressed about it.

That's the first part of the story. Why was Janice letting Paul tell her what was right and wrong? Because he presented a clear, powerful vision on the subject, confident that he knew best. Furthermore, this was a pattern in the rest of their marriage. Paul was the expert on many aspects of Janice's life, such as money, friends, and family. She felt he must be right even when he was ignorant, as with homosexuality.

I learned about this when the couple came to me for sex therapy about a year later, which is the second part of the story. The complaint was Janice's low sex drive. My diagnosis after two sessions was that "This isn't a sex problem. It's a relationship problem, an imbalance of power. Janice has no other way of asserting her independence or needs," I told them. "The low desire is also an effective way of avoiding criticism." It was only after we worked together for several months that Janice revealed her original secret. As soon as she did, everything made sense.

Janice's sexual secrecy was part of a larger relationship dynamic. Trying to tidy up your past in order to satisfy someone else's expectations is a common strategy, but it's not a good idea. It leads to resentment or unconscious feelings that come out later.

Our culture promotes rigid ideas about the meaning of the past and our responsibility regarding it. Most of us never think about society's attitude concerning people's pasts. Some of the contemporary messages are:

- The past is the best predictor of the future
- Many things done in the past are unforgivable
- Unless people repent, they should be expected to repeat their past behavior
- Despite repenting, some people still should not be fully forgiven
- It's always easy to know what to do; one can always avoid making mistakes

What a harsh, cold world such beliefs describe, lacking any sensitivity to the normal ways people change and grow. Most of us go through larger-scale changes, such as adolescent sexual awakening and mid-life reassessment. People also experience a wide range of gradual, less dramatic ones, which we don't realize at the time. I hear these changes described in many ways, including, "It stopped being fun," "I began to realize I was actually attractive," "I suppose I outgrew it," and "Maybe I just got tired of the hassles."

Living in a society that refuses to recognize the reality of normal change leads many people to believe that their past marks them forever. They feel it reflects on who they are now, rather than on who they were then. A healthier attitude would involve renouncing this belief and accepting the parts of our past we like least, saying, "I wouldn't do that again now, but it was right for me at the time."

Our society's beliefs about individuals' pasts is, for the most part, hypocritically unforgiving. Pejorative terms like "illegitimate child," "unwed mother," "ex-con," "promiscuous," and "unnecessary abortion" cast people in stereotypes, discrediting their choices and ignoring the human drama behind them.

The government is also guilty of this. The House Un-American Activities Committee, for example, was convened in the 1950s to hound people about their behavior in the 1930s. The transcripts clearly show committee members lacked any sense that people change over time.

I suppose we cannot be shocked about such weakness. As *Tristram Shandy* author Laurence Sterne said a century ago, "Only the brave know how to forgive." As for the very un-Christian lack of forgiveness in our civilized culture, novelist Dame Rose Macaulay said it best the year before she died: "Most of my friends are not Christians, although I have some who are Catholics or Anglicans."

According to modern custom, there are some pasts that you shouldn't, indeed, probably couldn't, forgive. We can see how this encourages sexual secrecy in a "case" from a TV soap opera.

I saw this little episode while delayed in the Seattle airport last year. Don't ask me which soap it was, because they all look alike to me. Jason and Robyn had recently become engaged. Overcome with happiness and feeling very close to Robyn, Jason said he wanted to tell her something.

JASON: Now that we're going to get married, I want to tell you all about me, even stuff from a long time ago. I certainly don't want you to find out certain things from someone else.

ROBYN: Like what?

JASON: Well, when I was in college I was a male stripper. I worked at sororities, bachelorette parties, that sort of thing. It got pretty wild sometimes. I guess some women think it's a big deal to hang out with entertainers.

ROBYN: You did what?! Jason, I'm surprised. And disappointed. It doesn't sound like you.

JASON: You're right, I feel embarrassed about it. It made sense at the time, but that part of my life is behind me now.

ROBYN: You sure? 'Cause lots of those college girls would still love to, uh, 'hang out' with you now, I bet.

JASON: Hey, don't tease me. Really, it was centuries ago. I just want you.

ROBYN: Okay. I love you.

JASON: I love you too. I'm glad I told you.

But in the following two scenes, the "real world" interferes:

JASON: . . . so I told her.

JASON'S FRIEND: You what?! That's crazy. She'll never let you forget it.

JASON: You don't know Robyn. She's very understanding. And she trusts me.

JASON'S FRIEND: You don't know women, my friend. You shouldn't have told her. She'll be suspicious forever.

ROBYN: . . . so he told me about his "Male Express" days.

ROBYN'S SISTER: God! So what'd you say?

ROBYN: That it was weird, but since it's obviously behind him, no problem.

ROBYN'S SISTER: Brave of you to put up a front.

ROBYN: Front? What are you talking about? I meant it.

ROBYN'S SISTER: Well, you certainly can't trust him now, if that's where he's been. You must have been shattered. You don't really believe he won't be tempted, do you? 'Cause when a man's tempted, that's that.

Jason and Robyn use their relationship as a resource. The way they handle this potential problem brings them closer together. It also helps motivate the next round of sharing and closeness. You can see how the attitude of their "friends," on the other hand, encourages secrecy, which frequently results in a mess later on. These friends haven't learned the advice Shakespeare gave in *Othello* over three hundred years ago: "To mourn a mischief that is past and gone is the next way to draw new mischief on."

A final cultural norm worth mentioning is "Blame the Victim." Loved ones of rape and incest victims sometimes feel so guilty or powerless that they blame the victim for not resisting enough. Insensitive people even wonder if the victim asked for it, or enjoyed it.

This kind of hostile ignorance encourages secrecy on the part of the victim. Indeed, the FBI estimates that only one out of ten rapes are actually reported. This is a dramatic example of how cultural attitudes encourage sexual secrecy.

HOW WE KEEP SECRETS ABOUT THE PAST

One of the commonest ways to keep secrets about the past is simply to lie.

Doesn't that bother people who think of themselves as moral and honest? Most certainly. "But Maureen was all ready to make unfair assumptions," said Arnold, a thirty-eight-year-old fashion designer. "I thought I'd spare us an unnecessary problem, so I justified lying by thinking about the satisfying relationship we were building."

Maureen, it seemed, was scared about getting AIDS. When she discovered that Arnold was in an industry with a large gay and bisexual population, she wanted to stop sleeping with him, at least until he got tested for the virus. Unwilling to deal with the issue, Arnold told her he had shifted into the field only recently, implying that he had never had sexual contact with other men.

"I only masturbated with a couple of guys a few times," Arnold told me. "Maureen had once called that 'gay sex,' putting her, she felt, at risk. I felt there was no risk, so I said I'd never done it. I just wanted us to move on and have a normal relationship."

For some people, keeping sexual secrets about the past involves destroying evidence, such as mementos. Gifts like paintings or books may also need to be given away, particularly if obviously selected by someone with taste much different from your own.

Recall our discussion about privacy: "I feel okay about this, and simply do not wish to share it" is different from, "These things are evidence of something bad that I've done."

Secret-keepers often have a distorted sense of what responsibility means. Thus I often hear something like, "George refuses to let me wear anything that other men have given me." Why should one person decide the boundaries of permissible privacy for the other? I call this "emotional fascism."

Another method of keeping secrets about the past is allowing or encouraging a partner's false assumptions. Because doing so does not involve outright lying, some people who use this strategy think they are being "pretty honest." It's a comfortable rationalization, but that's all it is. Sort of like being "somewhat pregnant."

The last kind of secret-keeping involves announcing some (unusual) behaviors in advance to be off-limits. "I don't do cunnilingus," a man might say, unwilling to examine why he might feel that way. "Call it weird if you like, but that's where I'm at. Subject closed." Here's an example of that:

Luanne and her fiancé, Ken, enjoyed sex with each other except for one major thing—he refused to give her oral sex. Since this was the easiest way for her to have an orgasm, she often felt disappointed. Frequently, one or both of them became angry about sex.

During their courtship Luanne tried various ways of interesting Ken in oral sex. But he always had some good reason for not doing it: his jaw was tired, he had a sore in his mouth, he didn't like her premenstrual smell.

Eventually, Luanne confronted Ken. "I don't think you'll ever go down on me," she yelled. Tired of the game too, Ken replied, "You're right. I never will. Now that's that. I don't want to discuss it again." He wouldn't explain why, and he had no suggestions as to how Luanne could increase his interest in it.

As I do with most couples, I had individual sessions with Luanne and Ken the week after they started joint counseling. Alone with me, Ken revealed his secret. Years ago he had been fairly clumsy the first time he made love, particularly with his oral technique. Unfortunately, the girl told some of her friends. One of them told her boyfriend, who used the information to humiliate Ken.

"I lost my stomach for oral sex after that," said Ken angrily. "I like intercourse a lot, but I won't repeat that scene," he declared. Why wouldn't he tell Luanne? "She wouldn't understand," he said. "Besides, it's too embarrassing," he offered more accurately. "Listen, this is just the way I am."

And that had become Ken's theme song: "I'm strange, and I won't communicate about being strange, but this is me. Take it or leave it." I saw Ken alone two more times. Not only did he refuse to talk about the oral sex issue, he became sullen and withdrawn whenever I focused on the relationship. I could neither reveal Ken's secret nor accomplish anything with him, so we ended treatment after a month.

THE SECRETS WE KEEP

There is an unlimited variety of secrets that people keep about their pasts. Part of the reason is the efficient way most of us are taught to criticize our sexuality. Another is the vast sense of permission our partners feel to criticize us.

But people shouldn't have to defend their past. Your past is part of you, and should be accepted as such. As Confucius said, "Things that are done, it is needless to speak about . . . things that are past, it is needless to blame."

Trust is an essential part of relationships. Your partner must trust that you have done your best at all times in the past. Only then can intimacy develop.

Be the custodian of your own past (and let others be the custodians of theirs). You shouldn't have to ask permission to do the things you already did years ago. You shouldn't have to tolerate a partner relating to the person you *were,* rather than to the person you *are.* Practice saying, "Apparently, I had to go through that to get to here. If you like me now, you need to accept the whole package."

Just as important, tell yourself the same thing—daily, if necessary.

Let us now turn to some examples of sexual secrets that people keep about the past.

"I'd rather Marc think I'm frigid than know I was raped," said June, a tall high school administrator. June avoided intercourse with Marc because it hurt so much, just as it did with the other two men she'd dated since being raped.

Why did she feel that way? "Because of the way Marc would probably react," she said. "I don't want his pity, and I don't want him wondering if I asked for it. It's just easier to keep it secret."

"That's true," I replied. Then I asked June to consider all the consequences of her secrecy. She felt isolated and angry. More important, she had compromised the integrity of her sexuality. I quickly added that I wasn't saying June *should* share her secret. I felt, however, she needed to be aware of secrecy's true costs.

"When the painful intercourse becomes totally unacceptable to you," I said, "sharing your secret, as part of working through the experience, will probably look like a sensible thing to do." The past will then no longer be something that owns June. It will simply be what it was: something that happened, "free of irrelevancies and loose ends," as Sir Max Beerbohm once said about the past.

Gary was hiding a different kind of past. The soft-spoken bus driver didn't quite know how to handle his experiences as a teenager.

"My first sexual encounters," he started after a long sigh, "were with my sister, who seduced me. I have mixed feelings about it—guilt because it was incest, but excitement when I remember how much she enjoyed it. I liked it, too, but I was more concerned about getting caught.

"She was much more mature than I was," he continued. "She was an old 16, I was a young 15. She talked me into it, saying she needed loving, but that she didn't trust the local boys. Then she wanted to do it again every few weeks. If I said no, she'd pout and say I didn't love her.

"Could a person who started this way have a normal sex life? I'm worried," Gary said with a choked voice. "I almost always date girls the opposite of my sister. She's short, with small features. But eventually they all remind me of her. That's when I worry about my erection, and usually stop having sex."

Gary's situation shows how hiding the past can keep it alive. Whenever Gary makes love, he is emotionally transported to the confusing times of adolescence. And the women he's with seem like his sister—powerful, seductive, and dangerous.

The message of Gary's secrecy is, "I did something bad in the past, which makes me a bad person now." He has no sense that the past and present are separate, and that the one cannot be judged with the logic, or hindsight, of the other.

Gary needs to decide that he is a normal, acceptable person with power of his own. Accepting his past would be an excellent way to do that. He could then think about how to handle the information with future partners. But revealing the secret is not the important thing. Accepting it is. Until Gary can do that, he will continue to have sexual difficulty.

As Sol Gordon gently puts it, "Why allow the ghosts of the past to determine what you can do today?"

Some people are unusually articulate about their secrets. Colleen, who became a prostitute before she was seventeen, told me, "It saved my life. I ran away from insane, brutal parents. Hooking was a way to make a living and feel appreciated. I even finished high school at night.

"But nobody understands that. They tell me I was a victim, or that my tricks were victims. A lot of people say prostitutes are dirty or evil. When I used to say, 'No, you're wrong,' they'd suspect I was into it, or was encouraging other girls to do it.

"So I don't tell them that anymore. I've made up an Aunt Addie who I spent '71 to '75 with. I stay with my story and keep the truth to myself. Wild horses couldn't drag it out of me, because I'm the one who'll get hurt."

Colleen may not feel guilty about the prostitution, but she does carry some baggage from it, which is the belief that relationships are temporary, at least for her. It reinforces the cruel lessons she learned as a child.

Unfortunately, hiding from judgment and misunderstanding can't help Colleen avoid her internal criticism. That's the voice that says, "Anyone who loves you must be some kind of loser." Colleen believes that if she cares about someone, she'll be left alone. Keeping secrets from those closest to her maintains that belief.

"Why do I mislead people about my past?" she asks rhetorically. "That's easy. People leave if you tell them the truth. Like that song says, 'Nothing in life is permanent; everything's on loan here.' Sure, some temporary relationships last longer than others. But what's the bottom line? Some famous guy once said, 'The only difference between blind lust and true love is that lust lasts a little longer.' "

Reclaiming your past is an important project. You can do it either by forgiving yourself or by deciding that there's nothing to forgive. Either way, you put the past behind you, which frees up your future. It also redistributes power in your relationships.

And if we don't do this? Almost half a century ago, Winston Churchill warned, "If we open a quarrel between the past and the present, we shall find that we have lost the future."

7

DELIBERATE DECEPTION

People lie for only one reason—fear of the loss of love.
— PROVERB

What a tangled web we weave, when first we practice to deceive.
— SIR WALTER SCOTT

Lying—that's what most people think I mean by this book's title. Here is the chapter where we discuss it.

WHY WE DECEIVE

There are four reasons that we deliberately deceive others about our sexuality:

1. Deception can be a response to the way we misjudge our sexuality, our relationships, and ourselves.
2. Deception can be a symbolic statement of other things.

3. Deception can be a way of transferring outdated childhood "truths" into adulthood.
4. Deception can be a way of overcoming our feelings of powerlessness.

Deceiving others almost always creates barriers. These barriers often stand between ourselves and other people. Equally important, they may also prevent us from seeing our own self-truths.

We have already seen how our childhood typically alienates us from sex and our bodies. This makes it difficult to evaluate accurately the true nature of our sexuality, or to anticipate others' reactions to the truth about us. These distorted perceptions make the truth look far more dangerous than it really is. Frequently, deception appears necessary when it is not.

Our estimates of the costs of lying are also distorted. We underestimate the stress produced by guilt, and the anger it generates in us. We underestimate the amount of psychic energy that deception requires, as we constantly monitor our words and actions lest we betray our secrets.

As one sadder-but-wiser client once told me, "One of the nice things about telling the truth is that there's nothing to remember."

A second reason we deceive is a symbolic one, relating more to secret-keeping than to the secret itself. For example, lying can be a subtle declaration that "No one can control me." Of course, feeling this way doesn't necessarily mean that your partner *wants* to control you. Perhaps it reflects your fear of closeness. Other people who feel they are being controlled are simply unaware of the amount of compromise required by healthy relationships.

In a similar way, some people use deception as a test. The unconscious dynamic is, "Look how bad I am. Do you still love me?" Another version is, "You say you want to be close to me? I'm going to make it very difficult. Let's see just how much you want to be close." The issue isn't whether or not the secret-keeper gets caught. It's the distance created by the deception that is paramount.

The third reason that people deceive sexually can be called "restimulation." It involves the way we sometimes experience old feelings in current situations, which leads us to act in the present as if it were the past.

Children who are constantly criticized, for example, learn to conceal anything that matters to them, such as their hobbies, their friends, their dreams, even their school successes. Such kids often grow up to be adults who only feel safe when they are hiding. They experience anyone interested in them as intrusive, overwhelming, and frightening. Secrecy often appears to be necessary for surviving adult relationships that feel like the dangerous ones of youth.

In many people, this dynamic is unintentional. But it can also be deliberate or calculated. One of Jonathan's experiences is a good illustration.

Although he started therapy because of job problems, Jon one day started talking about sex. That week his girlfriend had accidentally seen him masturbate for the first time, and observed him rubbing his breasts and pinching his nipples. When they made love the next day she repeated the caresses, but he abruptly pushed her away. "Don't touch me that way," he said roughly. "What kind of guy do you think I am?"

Jon was ashamed that he enjoyed having his breasts stimulated, unaware that many other heterosexual men enjoy it (according to Levine & Barbach, as well as Hite). Although he misled Sarah about it because he was afraid she'd laugh at him, there was a bigger issue. The closeness with her was just too threatening.

Jon was an only child, born after his mother's second miscarriage. Worried about losing him, too, his parents smothered Jon with well-meaning concern. To survive their constant fussing and questioning, Jon created an inner world of his own, shutting them out with long periods of contented silence.

Long years of protecting himself from others led to Jon's present personality. As an adult, his sexual secrets create the distance he needs to feel safe with his girlfriend. At thirty-three, Jon is still trying to create a safe childhood for himself.

Finally, deliberate deception can also be an expression of powerlessness, a common feeling in many relationships. When people feel appropriately powerful—to be heard, to change the rules, to get appreciation—deception is unnecessary. But there are many ways in which we may feel powerless with a spouse, parent, child, sibling, or close friend. Some thoughts and feelings that express this sense are:

- "I can't seem to get your attention."
- "There seems to be no way to change the rules around here."
- "There seems to be no way to make this relationship more satisfying for me."
- "You've said (or implied) that I can't talk about certain things I feel or want to do."
- "I feel outside forces requiring me to do this activity that we've agreed I won't do."

Such feelings can lead to deception—that is, breaking one or more parts of a relationship contract—as a person feels that staying within the contract's bounds doesn't work any more. While deceiving someone may look like an act of defiance or the assertion of power, it may actually be an act of fear, desperation, or frustration.

Mick had been married for fourteen years, enduring it rather than enjoying it. His wife, Tara, was always depressed. She couldn't handle housework, and she didn't want a job. Worse still, she didn't want to discuss Mick's unhappiness.

"I love her, and want to stay with her," the computer salesman said sadly, "but she just refuses to make an effort.

What am I supposed to do? Talking doesn't work, nagging doesn't work, pleading, threatening, and ignoring her don't work."

Eventually, Mick started sleeping with a Midwestern client he saw each month. A classic "I'll-do-anything-I-want" move? I don't think so. "I felt totally boxed in," Mick told me soon after it started. "I hated where I was and there was no way out. Tara said she had no energy for my 'demands.' I had to have contact with someone, so I let this affair happen. I feel like a person again. And, of course, guilty as hell."

Mick, I'm certain, would rather be talking, laughing, and making love with his wife. But he feels totally powerless to arrange that. He has not been able to find a way to join with Tara in joint problem-solving. And since Tara refuses to get either individual or marital counseling, there isn't much that can be done to heal the situation.

FEELINGS ABOUT DECEPTION

Most people have two different kinds of feelings about their deception. One is short-term and self-centered, almost childlike. You may have felt this in one or more ways:

- "I'm glad I'm doing this. It's about time I stood up to her/ him."
- "Finally, I'm doing something for me."
- "I'm not responsible, because I've been pushed to this."
- "I have to do this; I have no choice."
- "I deserve this, and I refuse to feel guilty about it."

I believe another set of more complex feelings lies underneath. While some people say they are completely unaffected by deceiving their intimates, I don't think that's true. In fact, the denial and blame behind such statements are part of the secrecy experience. People must do something, psychologically, to normalize their deception—that is, to deflect their guilt, shame, and self-criticism.

Somewhere in their psyches, almost everyone seems to have the sense that deceiving an important other is wrong. Is it ethics—or is it the memory of having been deceived ourselves? You can surely recall how you felt when you discovered yourself deceived: betrayed, humiliated, ashamed, angry. Although we may not think about these feelings often, they lurk in the mind's shadows, whispering.

So secret-keepers have a conflict. The inner child says deception is necessary, while the inner parent condemns it. The clash between these two sets of feelings often results in depression or anger. The depression leads to isolation, while the anger leads to blaming others.

In either case, the result is generally an adversarial relationship, experienced in feelings such as, "It's me against you," or "Either you're the problem or I'm the problem," or "You're not a resource, you're an obstacle."

This adversarial dynamic is a wound that must be healed before any other healing or change can occur. Unfortunately, people usually try to solve their problems without addressing the pain of being adversaries first. Such efforts typically succeed only at great cost, if at all. Sometimes they make the problem worse.

Acknowledging this win-lose attitude is important for two reasons. First, it helps people look at inner conflicts about their own behavior. Second, it creates the possibility of change that is more than cosmetic or temporary. Allowing an adversarial relationship to continue is to let the seeds of future bitterness lie in the ground, germinating.

Beneath both the childish and the parental feelings about deception is a pretense of powerlessness. The deceiver is convinced he or she has acted out of necessity: "I was pushed to it, I had to have the gratification." And the voice of guilt and shame says "I'm a bad person, too weak to resist."

But you can see deception differently—as active, not as reactive.

THE ACTIVE NATURE OF DECEPTION

While it is often easy to see another's deceptions as subtle forms of control or power, it is much harder to see our own deceptions that way. It is, however, important to realize that deception is a choice, and to take responsibility for that choice.

Doing so can help you deal with deception's consequences, both intended and unintended. Furthermore, because taking responsibility is an act of reclaiming your power, it can also help expand the range of options you perceive in a given situation.

You can see that deception is an active choice in several other ways. For example, deception frequently maintains a relationship's status quo by making it more bearable. Thus, if the relationship survives the early stages of deception, the system often becomes more stable, not less. A predictable dance of deception develops, in which all participants know their roles.

The system is also more stable because of a strange kind of accommodation. Deception can stretch a relationship to create possibilities not otherwise available. A common example is rules that frustrate you ("Don't do it"), combined with an activity that satisfies you ("I'm doing it"). The combination often proves irresistible to some people, although costly in the long run.

Deception, with its denial and blame, prevents people from identifying and healing the real problems that exist between them. Everyone considering secrecy needs to acknowledge this as part of their decision-making.

Deception is a dynamic tool of evolution, modifying any relationship it touches. Several of the following typically occur:

- You're not present and involved in quite the way you appear to be
- You cannot fully share yourself
- You're on guard
- Your partner, in some ways, becomes the enemy
- The scope of the shared vision of the future is reduced
- Resources are being drained, instead of being multiplied through collaboration
- You are creating the relationship's future primarily on your own, instead of jointly creating it with your partner
- The relationship may now include a third party. Whether it does or not, the deception itself is a third party in the relationship, the same as alcohol, overwork, or compulsive gambling can be.

Those being deceived often say that the most damning part is being unaware of participating in this new, revised relationship. Needless to say, these partners haven't given permission for the change.

Why don't we acknowledge the active nature of deception? Perhaps it's our hesitation to take responsibility for risky or ethically questionable behavior.

RELATIONSHIP AND CONTRACT ASPECTS OF DECEPTION

"People Don't Have Affairs, Relationships Have Affairs" was the title of an article I wrote for *Woman's World* in 1983. So too, deception isn't simply imposed by one person on another. It's imposed by one person on a relationship.

Deception specifically excludes your partner from efforts to solve a problem or nurture yourself. This is exactly the opposite of intimacy, particularly when your need for support arises from the partner or relationship itself.

We've discussed relationship "contracts" several times in

this book. They are the agreements, usually unspoken, that two people make about acceptable behavior and the penalties for unacceptable behavior.

Deception almost always violates a relationship contract. How?

- It involves "prohibited" behavior. An example is the use of birth control pills after agreeing not to.
- Deception itself is prohibited behavior, regardless of the content of the deception. An example is something as trivial as kissing a co-worker at her office birthday party, and then denying it later.

I assume that people do not break their agreements lightly. Why, then, do so many of us violate our relationship contracts periodically? Here are several common reasons:

- Indifference: we don't care about the relationship or our contract
- Denial: we deny that our behavior is truly a violation of our agreement
- Enmity: consciously or not, we feel that our partner is an adversary
- Powerlessness: we don't realize we have enough power to get what we want in other ways
- Fear: we're afraid that the consequences of not deceiving will be even worse

Wherever there is intimacy, or the desire for it, there is also fear of commitment. Our fear tempts us, consciously or not, to deceive as a way of creating a boundary or barrier between ourselves and others.

COMMON SUBJECTS OF DECEPTION

In this section we examine some common subjects of deception.

Extra-marital sex

The most talked-about deception, and the one that causes the most relationship problems by far, is extra-marital sex.

Surveys by *Psychology Today, Cosmopolitan,* and *Playboy* suggest that "affairs" occur in at least half of all American marriages. Comedian Jackie Mason has an even higher estimate: "Three-quarters of today's men cheat in America," he says. "The rest go to Europe."

The results of magazine behavior surveys contrast sharply with the results of opinion surveys such as the recent California Poll. When asked what contributes most to a successful marriage, the answer most often given was "sexual fidelity."

How can we account for this contrast? Why are so many people willing to invest the time and energy necessary to deceive their partners in this way when there is a general consensus that doing so is wrong? We might also ask the question in another way. If affairs are so common, why are they formally condemned by almost everyone?

In her book *The Extramarital Connection,* Lynn Atwater suggests that, "We are sexual schizophrenics. We say one thing and do another. We are still emotionally attached to traditional beliefs of sexual exclusivity, while we live with the needs and desires provoked by contemporary values which hold sexual expression to be a new social frontier."

I believe she is right. Our traditions about exclusivity date from an era of short marriages (due to short lives), rigid sex roles, and almost no privacy or personal time. We have yet to adjust our ideas to the modern reality of long life (which leads to long marriages), more flexible options, and extraordinary amounts of personal space and time.

Approaching the issue psychologically, we can see the clandestine relationship as a perfect recapitulation of childhood's drama. The person having an affair is, symbolically, hiding a treasure from Mommy or Daddy. The secret affair repeats the exciting, dangerous secret of childhood sexuality that we hid so well from our parents. This helps explain why affairs are so universally condemned, and yet still enjoyed.

But this is only part of the explanation. Other contemporary reasons for the high incidence of extra-marital affairs include:

1. *The expectation of personal fulfillment.* As Judith Bardwick notes in *In Transition,* the idea that people should be personally fulfilled beyond seeing their families grow and serving their God is new and radical. In fact, we really don't know yet if widespread "happiness" is possible over a long period of time. Frequently, an extra-marital affair is part of the search for that elusive fulfillment. Typically, however, this search is more effective when directed inward rather than outward.

2. *Our exaggerated notions of sexual satisfaction.* Until a century ago, very few people spoke openly about sex, and there were few sexually explicit materials available to common folks. The modern accessibility of sexual information and artistic expression is cause for celebration, but we should also be aware of its disadvantages.

One is the exaggerated picture most people have gotten of "good sex." Magazines, literature, well-meaning gossip, X-rated materials, and even some thoughtless self-help books have given people the idea that if they find the right partner, they can have the ecstasy of endless multiple simultaneous effortless orgasms.

In reality, good sex under the best circumstances is relatively brief, somewhat repetitive, and rarely mind boggling. It's great for what it is, but in the final analysis, sex is just sex.

3. *The cultural norm that non-marital sex is better.* One of the startling things that Hugh Hefner's *Playboy* did three decades ago was formalize and promote the idea that wives were boring. Times have changed since then, of course. Magazines now tell us that husbands are boring too.

The common media portrayal of marital sexuality ranges from perfunctory to nonexistent. Less than 10 percent of the sex presented on television, for example, takes place between married people. The exciting sex in romance novels is generally between women (married or not) and strangers.

A natural result of this is that people turn to other partners. Comedian Buddy Hackett best represents this position when he says that if you want to read about good sex and marriage, you have to buy two separate books.

4. *The routinization of marital sex.* Habituation is inevitable in long-term relationships. Routinization, however, is not. Consider the way most people prepare for sex with a non-spouse. The special underwear, perfume, teasing, little notes, setting aside time, and anticipation enrich extra-marital sex tremendously.

That kind of attention would improve the sex in almost anyone's marriage, making an affair seem much less "necessary." People who do not wish to make this investment always have "good" reasons to believe it would be fruitless. Often, the true reason is that they don't want to increase the intimacy in their marriage.

5. *The modern commitment to career.* In the old days, most paid jobs were dirty, tiring, and often dangerous. Today's careers are different. While work is still tiring, many of us also expect it to be stimulating, rewarding, and a vehicle for self-expression. Thus, many people today give their best thinking, sharing, listening, and creativity to their colleagues, who are doing the same. In some ways, many of us are now at our most attractive at work, rather than at home.

Our co-workers also seem to understand our concerns

and our language better than our spouses. When we add the fact that workplaces are now mixed-gender, we can understand how many affairs get started.

A FINAL NOTE ON AFFAIRS

Perhaps you are wondering why this book has no separate chapter on extra-marital affairs. It is because affairs are just like other secrets; they are primarily an expression of feelings about ourselves or our relationship. The majority of affairs are about attachment rather than sex.

True, affairs are a way for some people with low-desire spouses to have more sex. But just as often, people report that the lovemaking at home is as good as it is in the affair.

Sensitive people know that "fidelity" refers to much more than sex. In fact, some intimate conversations are far more of an infidelity than lovemaking would be. So this book treats affairs like any other secret. There is no separate chapter on affairs because affairs are rarely a separate chapter in people's lives. They are, more commonly, part of a theme woven through the special book we each write during our lifetime.

Faking orgasm

Why do women fake orgasms? First we must understand why they don't have orgasms. One reason is inner conflict about sex. Having been taught to be "good girls"—that is, non-sexual—adult women often have difficulty finally letting go and surrendering to their sexual feelings. As sociologist Carol Cassell says, it helps if you can claim you were "swept away"—by love, for example, or alcohol.

The second barrier to having orgasms is performance pressure, fostered by the belief that orgasm proves a woman's sexual competence. The third reason is the myth that women should climax from intercourse. Yes, it is a myth. Only 30 percent of the women surveyed for the 1976 *Hite Report* had orgasms from intercourse alone.

But why should women who don't have orgasms fake them? For the most part, they do it to satisfy their partners. As Shere Hite reported in her followup survey of seven thousand men, "The overwhelming majority of men realized that women often did not orgasm during intercourse, and found this a source of pressure. Many felt it was their fault." That's why men so often pressure women by asking, "Didja come?"

A few men also fake orgasms. I remember one friend's college experience of talking a young woman into having sex with him, and deciding about halfway through that it was a mistake. Instead of discussing things with her, he simply pretended that he was satisfied rather quickly, and followed with a hasty exit. Some men also pretend to enjoy their orgasm far more than they actually do.

Faking an erection, of course, is quite difficult, but some men with chronic problems do act surprised when they can't get an erection or when they lose it almost immediately. For some men, feigning shock is easier than talking about the problem honestly.

STDs (Sexually Transmitted Diseases)

No one used to inquire about the genital health or history of a partner; it was considered unnecessary and unromantic. Because of the AIDS, herpes, warts, and chlamydia epidemics, however, it is now necessary (although still, unfortunately, considered unromantic), so a few brave souls are asking questions. But most are not. Hope has always been a popular means of contraception but people are now trying to use it to prevent disease—and finding that it fails as preventive medicine as much as it always has as a contraceptive.

Unfortunately, you may not get an honest or dependable answer even if you do ask. Some people don't really know if they have, or have been exposed to, anything. Worse, some people do know, and are unwilling to tarnish their sexual attractiveness with the truth. They don't bring up the subject, and if you do, they lie.

There is no easy way of knowing how much you should rely on a partner's description of his or her sexual health. Only real familiarity, the kind that requires lots of time together, can provide helpful clues. Until you develop that closeness with a new friend, you might want to limit your relationship to mutual masturbation or tennis.

Same-sex experimentation

Because of AIDS, some people are screening potential lovers for bisexual experiences. As a result, some people with such backgrounds are deliberately misleading new partners.

I think, however, that there's more to it. According to sexologists like Dr. Charles Moser and Dr. Jack Morin, most true bisexuals are comfortable with their orientation. But some heterosexuals who have had a same-sex fling or two are troubled about theirs. Believing (correctly) that they're straight, they have trouble integrating these other experiences. They're afraid they're bi or, worse—"latent homo." Partly to deny this fear, they lie about themselves.

These people don't know what the Kinsey study found, and what countless surveys confirm. Almost half of American men and almost a quarter of American women have at least one same-sex experience as adults. They are still heterosexual.

Dislike

"I don't like the way you touch me or make love." I believe this is such a crucial piece of information that anything other than saying it plainly and clearly counts as deliberate deception. Do you fall into this common category? For a refresher on the subject, see Chapter 4 on arousal and response.

Sexual appetite

Western culture has traditionally pretended that women dislike and thus avoid sex, and that men are always interested in it. This belief is alive and well in modern America, as illustrated by this popular but biased joke:

A man wakes his wife at 3 A.M., saying, "I brought you two aspirin and a glass of water." "For what?" demands the sleepy woman. "For your headache," he replies. "You're crazy," she says, "I don't have a headache." "Finally!" exclaims her husband. "Let's make love."

To get a clear picture of the imbalanced expectations this joke presents, read it again with the wife waking the husband. In our culture, that version wouldn't be considered funny.

With these images so clearly defined, people often conceal their level of sexual interest if it runs counter to stereotype. Fearing criticism, some women conceal their hearty sexual appetite. Some men, on the other hand, hide their relatively low appetite, often with excuses or nitpicking.

People deceive their partners this way because they believe there is a "right" or "normal" level of sexual desire. But normal desire isn't a specific amount, it's a *range*. And it's a much wider range than most people realize. If you are not comfortable with your sexual appetite, you can productively seek help to change it. You should know that most people who enter therapy with desire problems are normal.

Another reason people deceive each other about their desire is because they're afraid of rejection. As we have already seen, this is usually based on a lack of self-acceptance. People who really accept themselves rarely worry about the dangers of being honest with other people.

Some women who feel their libido is abnormally low, for example, disguise this during courtship for fear of discouraging suitors. After marriage, they feel safer revealing their true interest level, which may clash with their husbands'. When the couple has recurring fights about sex, the woman can feel justified in her deception: "I knew sex would be a problem if I told the truth."

How much is absolutely too little desire? Joan Rivers

says it's if you go so long without sex that you forget who ties up who. What's too much? That's if you die of malnutrition because you don't stop lovemaking long enough to eat once a day.

Sex with a taboo partner

As we have already seen, not all secrets are kept from spouse or lover. Some are kept from friends and relatives. Consider the taboo partner: the sister, friend, son, ex-husband, rabbi, etc., of someone you know. We keep the relationship secret because we imagine terrible consequences from telling the truth. This may be a rational judgment. Then again, it may be the Secrecy Imperative's distortion.

We could avoid a lot of trouble with some straight talk. A woman might say, "Dad, your golf partner has asked me out and I just wanted to tell you myself before you heard it through the grapevine." Or your friend might say, "Janice, I know you're close to your brother's ex-wife. I'd like to start seeing her, and figured we ought to discuss it first." This is *not* the kind of grown-up conversation you hear on TV.

It would be interesting, in passing, to look at why people get involved with taboo partners. For some, the taboo itself is attractive. Consciously or not, the behavior says, "I can do whatever I like. I won't let logic or others' feelings stop me from seeing anybody I want."

People use these risky or forbidden relationships for other, often unconscious purposes as well. These include expressing revenge, anger, or sadness. Sometimes the desired result is disrupting the relationship that your new partner is having with a roommate, ex-lover, or co-worker.

Finally, people use taboo partners to create the next chapter in their ongoing script of "Love Never Works Out For Me." I'm delighted to tell the story of a patient who just recently interrupted such a pattern.

Twenty-eight-year-old Ron had been in therapy about a month. He was depressed, had little self-confidence, and no women friends. "Oh, Juanita asked me out today," he said one afternoon. "That's my brother's ex-wife. We've been friends for years. I'm not sure she's really done with him, but she says she is. It will be nice to cuddle with her. She's really nice."

The more Ron talked, the more Juanita looked like an accident just waiting to happen. She had started to call him at work almost every day, chatting casually even when he said he was busy. She mentioned fantasizing about them getting married. She wanted to be happy again, "like I was with Bruce."

I asked Ron what he intended to do. "Well, I hate to keep secrets from my family, but I don't think anyone would understand. I'll have to keep this quiet for a while." And what were his plans? Did he see himself marrying her? "No, I don't think she's right for me. Besides, the family gatherings would be really awkward."

I had Ron fantasize what it would be like: how he'd feel deceiving his brother, and later, ending the romance with Juanita when he met someone more eligible for marriage. Neither felt very good. "But what can I do?" Ron asked.

We approached it from another direction. "If the future consequences of a current decision look unacceptable, decide there are alternatives—and then find them," I said. Ron was intrigued. "You mean this could be a mess that I actually avoid!" he said excitedly. It's a concept he already understood about work, but not about love.

Ron realized he didn't have to be a person whose romances never worked out. Instead, he became a person who chose his romances carefully, so they had a good chance of being satisfying.

Lest we get too serious here, let's mention a few other common deceptions a little smaller in scope. How many of these do you keep from your mate?

- I like to touch your underwear
- I like to wear your underwear
- I like the noise you make during sex
- I masturbate looking at your picture or thinking about you
- I wonder if I'm normal (and maybe even think that *that's* not normal)

Perhaps you deceive friends or others with mini-secrets:

- I have no interest in women other than my wife (men rarely admit this to each other)
- I love being held down during sex
- I imagine you're a better lover than I am
- I'm embarrassed to teach my kids anything about sex

We have examined the various sexual secrets people keep. We've also talked about the conflicting feelings that often accompany deception. Since people frequently handle this conflict by pushing away their partners, deception often creates situations that demand further deception. This is a common way that we relinquish our personal power.

In the next section, we'll look at the process of decision-making. Everyone wants to make decisions that lead to happiness and closeness. Let's look at how you can improve your judgment about when and how to keep, and reveal, your sexual secrets.

PART III

TO SHARE
OR NOT
TO SHARE

Parts I and II have helped you raise important questions about your sexuality and relationships. In Part III, you will begin to develop answers to these questions so you can decide what you want to do about them.

Part III offers criteria for judging healthy and unhealthy reasons for sharing, as well as realistic and unrealistic goals. And, through helpful questions and gentle encouragement, it will help you uncover your real reasons and goals for sharing or not sharing.

This self-knowledge can be elusive, because when our motives are not pure and wholesome, we often hide them from ourselves. Yet this information is an important element in making peace with our sexual selves.

So, think of this section as an honest, dependable friend, someone who can help you see beneath your conscious attitudes and behaviors to what's really going on in your mind. You may not always like what this friend helps you see, but you value him or her for being willing to push you a bit toward recognizing your own best interests.

Part III will also help you evaluate the consequences of both sharing and secrecy. Anticipating these can be difficult for two reasons. First, we may not want to see certain consequences, because doing so would force us to choose a course of action that is frightening or intimidating.

Second, the act of choosing itself may flood us with guilt or other feelings because of the belief that consciously thinking about secrecy and sharing is not appropriate.

Regardless of your choice, I support you in your decision-making. Consciously making choices, in contrast to passively playing the role of victim, is a positive step. As the rest of this book has done, Part III will support you, reflecting these principles:

- Choosing how much you are willing to share is a continuing process, not a single event
- This choice should be made consciously
- You should understand the criteria you use to make your choices
- Neither secrecy nor sharing can be assumed to be best in any situation; every circumstance must be judged individually
- Since we all make assumptions about our sexuality and our relationships, these assumptions should be reexamined periodically

In Part III, there are separate chapters about sharing and non-sharing. This is to help you think about the legitimacy of each one. The chapters are, however, similar in many ways because they grow from the same ideas about closeness, personal power, and sexuality.

Dealing with the issue of conscious sharing involves no less than an examination of your most important inner pictures. What is your relationship? What is your sexuality? How much responsibility do you want to take for each?

Simply acknowledging these questions is a serious enterprise. Answering them is even more serious. Your willingness to enter this process deserves respect and appreciation— so regardless of where your journey goes, you have mine.

As you approach the last third of this book, take advantage of the depth of its support. Nurture yourself by letting yourself be nurtured.

8

WHEN
SHOULD
YOU SHARE?

Though I am not naturally honest, I am so sometimes by chance.

—WILLIAM SHAKESPEARE
The Winter's Tale

This is the chapter in which you will explore the decision to share sexual secrets. We'll discuss the issues involved, and look at how you can evaluate yourself and your relationships in terms of those issues. By the end of the chapter, you should be able to make an informed judgment about sharing one or more secrets.

Most decisions to keep secrets are not clearly thought through. As explained in Part I, secrecy often develops unconsciously, appearing uninvited in adult relationships. When secrecy is chosen consciously, it is frequently a response to some kind of fear.

Either way, you may now be considering a change. Perhaps you have come to understand the consequences of your secrecy in a new way. Perhaps your needs have changed over time.

Choosing to share your secrets makes sense when you have both 1) a good reason for doing so, and 2) sufficient resources to handle the results.

Let's look at each of these.

HEALTHY GOALS OF SHARING

When partners in healthy relationships feel angry, scared, confused, humiliated, sad, or lonely, they can simply say so. When they do, they expect to be heard. For many people, this is a radical concept.

A good relationship provides alternatives to expressing these feelings by hostile or manipulative sharing. Sharing a secret isn't something you do *to* someone. Rather, it is something you do *with* someone, enhancing intimacy or self-esteem.

But this can be tricky. For example, the following disclosures would, in most circumstances, be hostile:

- "I think of your sister when we make love."
- "I had much better orgasms with that one-night stand last year."
- "Mom, let me tell you all the details about having sex with my boyfriend."
- "Before you leave me, I want you to know that I've been having an affair."

Now, some constructive aspects of sharing secrets:

- The sharing specifically addresses the effects of secrecy on the secret-keeper and/or the relationship
- The sharing doesn't manipulate or mislead the partner
- The sharing contributes positively to the health of the secret-keeper and/or the relationship

From this list, we can decide that the following are good reasons for sharing secrets. When you share in good faith, under the right circumstances, the goals below are possible and healthy:

- Getting closer to your partner
- Improving your sexual relationship
- Increasing your self-esteem
- Reducing the physical or emotional stresses of secrecy
- Changing a relationship, or supporting a current change

Let's look at these in detail.

Getting closer

Sharing can bring two people closer by helping them understand each other. True, your partner may disagree with your perceptions, be disappointed by your feelings, or not want to give you what you want. At the very least, however, he or she will have a better sense of what the world looks like through your eyes.

Sharing can provide "the missing link." As one husband told me about his wife's sharing, "I didn't like what I heard, but I was glad I heard it. Even though I don't know what to do about it, at least now I know why she avoided making love."

Even if sharing only lets a partner know that you feel ashamed or angry, it can still make a difference. You may not see the positive effects right away, but they will appear eventually. The changes may not even appear in a sexual form, but rather in a related area, such as the balance of power, the way you talk to each other, or just the way you feel when you're together.

When people share strong feelings and emotional experiences, even painful ones, they often become closer. You may, for example, feel the exhilaration of taking risks by revealing yourself or thinking about your relationship in new ways. Or you may feel the excitement of having your secrets greeted and accepted. Or you may feel the pleasure of seeing your partner's emerging self-esteem.

Sometimes revealing a secret involves sharing pain. People often feel sad about having kept part of themselves hidden. The sharing partner may feel ashamed or embarrassed. At the same time, sharing the secret may also include recognizing the partner's pain. He or she will probably feel bad about having been deceived, or about having encouraged the deception unknowingly.

Finally, sharing can also include a mutual acknowledgment that this is a moment of transition. You and your mate may feel proud of your relationship. You may appreciate its resources, or you may both worry that more change is coming, fearing that it will be difficult to handle.

In all these ways, the strong emotions surrounding sharing can bring partners closer together. Whether it's a devastating tornado or a million-dollar lottery win, powerful experiences always offer this opportunity.

Making sex more satisfying

The desire to improve your sexual relationship is another good reason to share sexual secrets. You may consider sharing a fairly easy step, or you may resort to it only out of desperation.

Some people decide to share secrets only after enduring unsatisfying sex for a long time. Others feel relatively satisfied, but discover or decide that more is possible. Such an awareness can come from a book, TV program, conversation, or even through an extramarital affair.

Sometimes we desire change after learning about ourselves. Lonnie Barbach and other therapists suggest masturbation as an excellent way for women to learn more about their sexual responsiveness. Women who have never experienced an orgasm before often do this way, opening the door for exploration with a partner.

Sharing can lead to better sex simply by allowing a person to be more relaxed. Remember "lights-out" Sandy from Chapter 4? Telling men the secret that she is embarrassed about her body would change sex for her dramatically. Lovemaking would no longer be a place where Sandy punished herself. Her partners would appreciate her body and give her positive feedback. She could be less self-conscious.

And, of course, sharing secrets—information—with partners gives them a chance to stimulate you the way you like. A man ashamed of wanting his buttocks caressed, for instance, might finally get to enjoy that without struggling with himself.

Happily, sharing is not all one-sided. Your sharing invites your partner's sharing, bringing many benefits for him or her. Peg and Irv, an older couple I worked with years ago, were retired teachers who enjoyed their marriage and led active lives. They had heard me lecture, and came to me for advice on several issues concerning their adult children and adolescent grandchildren.

Our sessions had an easy, comfortable feeling. At one point I gave Peg a few of my magazine articles to share with her daughter. The following session she looked more serious than usual.

"Irv, one of these articles got me thinking," she announced after we all sat down. "I know you love me and want to give me pleasure, but it's time to tell you that sexually, I've changed. A powerful penis banging into me just isn't my first choice anymore."

Irv's face was a mixture of worry, affection, and excitement. "You mean I don't have to do the old battering ram routine all the time? That's great!" he said, to Peg's surprise. "I'm not as young as I once was either, you know." Her sharing had encouraged his.

As they realized they'd each been accommodating what they thought the other wanted, they began laughing. The truth is, intercourse had become a lot of work. They both preferred mouth or hand stimulation. But Peg didn't want to hurt Irv's pride as a lover, and Irv didn't want Peg to feel she didn't turn him on anymore.

"Now let's not forget intercourse altogether, right?" Peg said playfully. Irv winked and nodded. If only therapy were always this satisfying, I thought.

Sometimes sharing enables you to satisfy your partner more. Take Lila and James, a fundamentalist Christian couple. They enjoyed their lovemaking together, but each admitted to me, in private, that it lacked a spark.

Lila was disappointed about several things, one of which was that she never had a chance to give James oral sex. "Have you ever suggested it?" I asked in our one-to-one interview. "No," she replied, "he's real Bible-minded. I'm afraid he'd think I'm a loose woman, and get nervous about my past."

In his private interview with me, James also expressed disappointment. "Lila's very loving, very giving," he said. "But I sure wish she'd go down on me." Surprise! I inquired if James had ever encouraged Lila, or asked her about oral sex. "No way," he said with feeling. "I wouldn't take a chance on offending her. She might not understand that it's a common, normal thing to do."

To start their joint session the following week, I said several pretty standard things. "Most mates," I started, "have secrets from each other. While privacy is crucial in relationships, some of that secrecy is unnecessary, even harmful. I never force anyone to reveal secrets, but if either of you wants to share anything, now is a good time."

The room was quiet. Then Lila turned to James and spoke. "I don't feel totally free," she said, "I'd like to . . ." She paused. "I'd like to please you in *different* ways." The words didn't come easily for Lila. She was frightened.

But she told him anyway. When James realized what Lila was saying, he was delighted. Lila was moved by her husband's acceptance. It was what the business school people call a win-win situation.

Increasing self-esteem

Enhancing or supporting self-esteem is another good reason to share sexual secrets. In a healthy partnership, each person is vitally interested in the self-esteem of the other. This makes secret-sharing a good use of the partnership's resources.

What is self-esteem? It is the sense of accepting yourself, regardless of what you do. But this sense does not come easily. Low self-esteem has its roots in early childhood, when we first experience our parents' criticism and appreciation.

Children vitally need to understand that although they may do unacceptable things, they themselves are acceptable. This acceptance leads to a deep sense that "I am okay." But as Swiss psychologist Alice Miller notes, parents tend to criticize children in terms of who they *are,* rather than in terms of what they *do.*

How many times have you heard a parent say, "You're a bad girl," instead of saying, "When you don't pay attention, it's easy to knock over your milk. You must pay closer attention." Or "Nice boys don't touch themselves" instead of "I know that feels good, but we don't touch our private parts in public. Let's wait till we get home, and you can do that in your room."

So most children learn the damaging lesson that if they *do* something bad, they *are* bad. They also learn (from parents who are otherwise quite loving) that they are "lazy," "sloppy," "mischievous," and so on, instead of learning that they are wonderful little people who sometimes do inconvenient, incorrect, or self-defeating things.

People who somehow develop high self-esteem are able to separate themselves just a bit from their victories and defeats. They may not like something they do, but they see no reason to stop liking themselves. And they don't exaggerate their successes, because their sense of self isn't based on individual accomplishments.

Healthy sharing is an expression of self-acceptance, and

thus of self-esteem. For example, sharing can help you maintain or strengthen your self-image as an honest person. This might be important after a particular event, or as part of some current growth process.

My neighbor Tom told me a great story about this once. "I've always believed myself to be pretty honest," he said, "More so than a lot of guys. One day my six year old asks me what a 'white lie' is. As I was telling him, I realized I'd been holding out on Rae [Tom's wife] for months. I didn't like a new way she was sometimes kissing me. I decided to tell her that very night. As a result, we had a great talk about a whole bunch of stuff."

For some people the stakes are much higher, which they often describe as "no longer wanting to live a lie." A man may finally tell his wife that he sometimes wears women's clothes. A woman may admit to her husband that she was sterilized before they met. For many, the exciting sense of self-acceptance following the disclosure outweighs virtually any difficulties sharing may bring.

Other secrets appear relatively minor to outsiders, but have strong meaning for the person involved. "Coming out" might include dressing so that a small bosom is no longer hidden; refusing to allow a lover's cat in the room during sex; and acknowledging having once seen and enjoyed an X-rated film.

Perhaps you have kept one or more sexual secrets because in the past your partner reacted to the truth harshly. (Note: We're talking about experience here, not just assumptions.) Sharing sexual secrets can support your decision to stop shying away from confrontation—which can have a dramatic impact on your self-esteem. Examples of assertive sharing might include talking about:

- Not having orgasms from intercourse
- Wanting to date others, or wanting to end a sexual relationship altogether

- Desiring oral sex
- Using erotic films in masturbation
- Masturbating as a married person

One thing I've told clients over the years is, "Once you decide that avoiding pain is your primary goal, you never get to make another decision." Avoiding confrontation is a full-time, emotionally costly job. Everything else becomes subordinated to it, requiring you to play perpetual catch-up and mind-read. Deciding to end the whole exhausting routine is a big boost to self-esteem.

Sharing also increases self-esteem in its inherent statement that "I am an equal." Many people live with imbalanced power arrangements, unaware that relationships can function any other way—or that change is possible. Sharing can be a powerful intervention in an otherwise unyielding situation.

The idea that what you want is as important as what your partner, parent, or child wants may be a radical, life-changing concept. It can rebalance the power in a relationship. Of course, this involves assuming responsibility for your own frustration, rather than blaming it on someone or something more powerful than you are. That can be both frightening and exhilarating.

Reducing the stresses of secrecy

Sharing is an important way to reduce the physical and emotional burdens of secrecy. Nothing illustrates this better than the story of a man I worked with about a year ago.

John was referred to me by a colleague at the University Sleep Clinic. He was having nightmares about twice a week, always with the same theme. "I'm so tired of being chased," the thirty-year-old father of twins told me. "Sometimes it's by Nazis, other times by escaped convicts, or the police. I always wake up running for my life."

I asked John about his family, job, and overall health, and gave him my intake form to complete. For the last question asked—"In one word, please describe your sexual relationships"—John's answer was "schizophrenic."

"It's great when I masturbate," he replied when I asked about this. "I have super fantasies about old girlfriends and I last a long time. But with my wife it's sort of dull. And I pretend to be more interested than I really am."

John's answer and his recurring nightmares could have meant many different things. But considered together, I felt they reflected feelings of stress and conflict. I asked John to tell me more about his secret.

"Well, I don't like hiding," he said sadly. "Or feeling like two different people." I asked how much he thought about getting caught. "I used to think about it a lot," said John, "especially after I heard a radio show one night saying that wives could tell when husbands were unfaithful." An interesting way to describe his secret life, I thought.

"I've just trained myself never to think about it," John continued. "I just enjoy what I've got and try to stay out of trouble."

I believe it's virtually impossible to ignore strong feelings. John's nightmares were starting to look like the product of repressed fear and guilt. "What would happen if you simply told Betty about your 'other life'?" I asked. John shuddered. "I couldn't," he said simply. "Besides, why would I admit something like that?"

It took a few sessions, but I finally helped John understand that masturbating was not bad, "even though" he was married. And I explained that wild fantasies are also normal. "Perhaps," I suggested, "your wife might be willing to come with you to counseling so that both of you can be more sexually fulfilled."

John wasn't ready for that, so we continued individual counseling. I remember him saying, about a month later, that

"Our talks about normality have given me a lot to think about." Two weeks after that, John said, "You know, I'm feeling great relief from these sessions. I didn't realize how uptight the whole thing made me. Oh, by the way," he added as our session ended, "the nightmares have just about stopped."

John still had not told his wife his secret, but he had come to accept it himself. For now, that was enough. He looked more secure and self-confident as he went to the door. His life had changed forever.

Creating or maintaining relationship change

Carefully planned sharing can be a way of creating change in your relationship. This can unfold in different ways. Winston, for example, was a construction worker who drank heavily. As soon as he came home from work he'd open a six-pack of beer "to relax." By half past eight he'd be asleep on the living room couch, six empty cans beside him. He and his wife Julie had practically no life together, and rarely enjoyed each other's company.

Julie had left him and returned twice. To complicate matters, they had an infant daughter. Winston refused to discuss his drinking at home or in our sessions, insisting he wasn't an alcoholic because he could quit anytime. Julie's pleas for a warmer relationship fell on deaf ears.

Desperate for a solution, Julie chose to force the issue by confronting Winston's male vanity. She brought a twelve-month wall calendar to our session, with three days circled in red.

"These are the three times we've made love this year," she announced, "and it's already October. We never have sex because you're either drunk or asleep. I've had two offers of affairs from men at work, and I'm considering which one to accept. Are you going to change and save our marriage, or shall we get a divorce?"

Winston accused her of bluffing, then of not understanding him, and finally of being a slut. "I read an article that says most couples under thirty have sex at least once a week," Julie countered. "Are you going to get normal or not?"

As Julie feared, Winston refused to acknowledge her pain, and refused to bond with her to save their marriage. But she finally had enough information, and was able to act. It was time for her to make the biggest change of all: separation and divorce. "It was the hardest thing I've ever done," she told me a year later, "but I've never regretted it."

Sometimes sharing leads to change that is just as drastic, but with a much different result.

A bookkeeper I worked with felt powerless in her marriage, which everyone else believed was perfect. While Dawn was able to tell her husband, Scott, that she was unhappy, somehow change never followed.

She eventually decided to use the issue of sex to make Scott understand her frustration. "We always do it your way," she said. "Always you on top, never me. Why can't we ever experiment?" she demanded. "I am very unhappy sexually. Did you know that?" Dawn had dropped the bomb.

"What's the difference what position we use?" Scott replied. "You usually climax, I last long enough, why do we have to mess around with things?" Dawn's face sagged as she met Scott's resistance. "I don't know what to say," she said to me, near tears. "He's right, as usual. Is there something wrong with me?"

I encouraged them to talk to each other more, but they kept returning to the same place, so I stepped in more actively. "Scott," I said, "Dawn would like things her way. You would like things your way. You seem to feel that a person only gets his way if he has a good reason. Is that accurate?"

Scott instinctively resisted this observation, saying he wanted Dawn to be happy. "I believe you really mean that," I said gently, "but does Dawn ever get her way when you don't feel she has a good reason?"

Scott named a few minor instances, but could not name

anything of importance. Suddenly, Dawn's face lit up. "It shouldn't be Scott's decision, should it?" she asked excitedly. "That's why I feel so crazy—I'm always having to defend myself, and Scott makes it sound normal."

"And what happens then?" I asked encouragingly.

"Sooner or later," Dawn replied, "it becomes easier to do what he thinks is best."

"And," I said, completing the picture, "Scott thinks you're doing what you want, while you don't understand why you're unhappy."

Scott and Dawn looked at each other thoughtfully. "I don't know what we should do," Scott said quietly, "but feeling this way is no good, is it?"

Without knowing it, they had just started to change their relationship.

Finally, sharing can support relationship or personal changes already in progress, an opportunity people frequently overlook. Let's say a man, through classes or reading, is becoming more assertive, a change his girlfriend likes. She can now share her secret—"I've wanted you to be more dominant in bed." Her sharing supports his change.

INAPPROPRIATE REASONS TO SHARE

Just as there are constructive reasons for sharing secrets, there are destructive ones as well. Sharing which is motivated by the wrong reasons is not likely to support the health of individuals or relationships. Instead, it often mobilizes a partner's anger, desire for retaliation, and vision of sex as a weapon.

Sharing for the wrong reasons is also a form of dishonesty. While the sharing transaction may *appear* to involve closeness or regret, it may really be a disguised expression of anger. Pretending to feel one way when you feel another is the classic definition of manipulation. As most television soap operas show, manipulation usually creates messy situations.

I strongly advise against using secrecy, surprise, or other dirty tactics to express strong feelings such as anger—even though at times we all feel like doing so.

Fighting dirty keeps us at the level of our childish, vulnerable feelings. This keeps us from feeling safe enough to address issues productively. In addition, partners frequently respond with dirty tactics of their own, which further removes everyone involved from the real issues.

If, on some level, you feel vengeful, proceed cautiously. What should you do if you feel like hurting or punishing your partner? Rather than doing it, tell him or her about *wanting* to do it. Say, for example, "Marge, when you flirt like that it makes me angry. Sometimes I feel like flirting with one of your friends just so you'll know how it feels. Or even telling you about some of my past exploits so you'll feel left out the way I do."

This is a more productive way of handling feelings, and in all but the worst relationships, it will get your partner's attention. Make sure your partner understands that the reason you're not acting out your feelings is because your concern for the relationship is bigger than your hurt.

If you are determined to hurt your partner, do it directly and explicitly. Say, for example, "You insist on telling me about your old girlfriends even though I've begged you not to. I think it's time you heard about some of my exploits." This will make it clear that punishment is on the agenda.

The following are common non-productive reasons for sharing secrets.

- To get revenge
- To punish or humiliate
- To relieve a heavy burden of guilt
- To invite criticism or punishment
- To test the relationship
- To create a smokescreen

Let's examine them in detail.

Revenge and punishment

"Life being what it is," said painter Paul Gauguin, "one dreams of revenge." The desire to punish others appears to be a natural human feeling. The question is whether or not you want to live with the consequences of pursuing those desires.

Here are a few ways that people sometimes punish others by sharing sexual secrets:

- The teenager who angrily tells her restrictive parents that she's been sleeping with her boyfriend for six months
- The woman who tells her critical husband that, far from being "frigid" as he accuses, she has a rich fantasy life
- The man who tells his father, at his mother's funeral, that she molested him as a child—and asks why his father didn't protect him

Revealing sensitive sexual material can be a self-destructive or self-defeating way to hurt others. First, you demean yourself by saying, in effect, "The truth about me is so ugly that I use it as a weapon."

Second, you create suspicion and damage your partner's trust in you, as he or she can now imagine you doing this again. And by showing that punishing-through-revealing is acceptable to you, you also open the door for your partner to use such behavior.

Finally, and most poignantly, using sensitive material to punish someone frequently fails to communicate how much and why you're in pain. The other person may be so angry, hurt, and confused that your unhappiness gets lost in the shuffle.

Relieving guilt

Relieving guilt is an inappropriate reason for sharing a sexual secret because it is an abuse of the relationship. I have,

I know, encouraged you to use your relationship as a resource, but there is a limit. You can determine what that is partly by examining alternative resources, such as your friends, pastor, or therapist.

Ask yourself, how much pain will this cause relative to the relief I receive? That is, how much of a problem will it create for my partner? If you're essentially trading your pain for your partner's, that's not fair.

Also, are you planning to do anything about your situation after your guilt is lifted? If not, you're just dumping your guilt on someone else without any productive outcome. This is selfish.

An example: A woman has an affair, feels guilty, and then tells her husband. The revelation is painful for both of them, but she feels better. Two months later she has another affair. Under these circumstances, I would say that sharing had been irresponsible and abusive.

In general, guilt is a destructive motivation. Guilt is not the same as a sense of fair play, or the desire to do the right thing, or an active conscience. It reflects the sense that "I am bad." Naturally, we all want the pressure of that feeling removed. But that's your problem, not your partner's.

This is one of those unusual cases where Ann Landers and I agree: relieving guilt is a destructive reason for sharing sensitive information, such as extra-marital affairs.

Therapist Fritz Perls believed that guilt and anger are closely connected. He observed that when you feel guilty—that is, critically judging yourself—you often lash out at someone you imagine to be judging you. One of the ways people do that is by revealing sexual secrets that hurt others.

Inviting criticism or punishment

Although they'd deny it if you asked, some people unconsciously seek out the criticism of others. Why? It fulfills some inner vision of themselves as worthless, troublesome, inept, or unloved. For example, I have seen extremely competent people become unaccountably clumsy, even spilling things on a hostess's gown, because they feel unworthy of the company.

Punishment also relieves people who fear they are out of control. It makes them feel controlled and therefore *cared for.* And it reassures them that they are needed by their partner, who is often a person who needs someone to control.

Unless the desire for criticism is extreme, we usually don't think of such people as "sick." In fact, we often compliment them for being modest, soft-spoken, and sweet. Many such "normal" people are simply afraid of their fantasies, thoughts, and impulses.

"Only I know how bad I really am," goes one unconscious belief. "At least this person is giving me the punishment I deserve, even if it's not for the right thing."

Testing relationships

Some people repeatedly test any relationship that seems too good to be true. They irritate a partner in order to see if he or she will leave when angry. Or they show and exaggerate their flaws and limitations early on to reduce their anxiety about eventually being rejected. "Reject me now," one client recently told me, "and avoid the holiday rush."

Rather than test our partners, we should give them a chance to negotiate, voice their own complaints, and discuss the issues involved. There is always the chance that they will wish to handle a conflict as our teammate rather than as an adversary.

Testing a relationship unannounced is also unfair because people are rarely at their best when surprised. People often feel threatened, and frequently act defensively or aggressively. But given the chance, the same people might be happy to negotiate an issue.

Psychologically testing a relationship, another common

conceit of soap operas, is a cowardly way of collecting information. And, as the soaps illustrate, you can't count on the quality of the information.

It's an insecure or unstable person who has to hide his or her motives in order to feel safe. If this really is the case, it should be discussed in the open, as it reflects a brewing crisis for individual and/or couple.

Smokescreens

Some people share with the intention of misleading a partner about the future. This includes people who plan on having affairs or on withholding further information about what turns them on or off. Planning future secrets is a cynical motive for sharing that calls into question a person's commitment to the relationship. Specifically, how can you be trusted as a partner? What is your word worth?

Deception is also the saddest of all reasons for sharing a secret. It means that you feel alone, abandoned by both partner and relationship. It means you anticipate that future hiding will be necessary. It means you've decided that you can't be yourself in this relationship. Thus, sharing for this reason is a clear signal that your relationship is in trouble.

EVALUATING YOUR MOTIVES

How can you be sure that one of these six inappropriate motives for sharing *isn't* on your agenda? After all, we may approach sharing in the kindest, most generous mood, and yet use it to manipulate or to express hostility.

Here are a few guidelines to help you evaluate your motives:

- Do you anticipate a partner's shock, surprise, pain, or resentment with delight or self-righteousness?
- Are you looking forward to an angry confrontation over what you are considering sharing?

- Do you feel angry or hurt as you prepare to share? Does the anger or hurt increase as you get closer to your decision?
- Are you already planning how you're going to get away with a future forbidden activity, planned or unplanned?
- Are you thinking about sharing just to see how your partner responds?
- Have you thought about with whom you will discuss the results of your sharing?
- Are you feeling like a bad child as you prepare to share?

Each "yes" answer suggests a non-productive motive. Think over this possibility carefully before proceeding further: What is your real agenda? Is there a more honest, more direct way to pursue it?

RESOURCES

Anyone can share a sexual secret. But doing it successfully—getting the results you want from sharing—requires resources, both personal and relational. These resources allow two partners to use the revealed information constructively.

Almost all human beings have difficulty handling sensitive issues. We express those difficulties through feelings like jealousy, fear, anxiety, and anger. Because of the power of these feelings, good will alone is often not enough to make sharing productive. What assets, then, should you look for as you decide whether or not to share?

Communication

The ability and willingness to communicate is certainly your greatest asset. Good communication enables couples to use their love, intelligence, shared history, and good intentions productively. Here are some guidelines for effective communication:

- We can listen without feeling attacked or criticized
- We can disagree without needing to destroy each other
- We can express anger fully without needing to hurt each other
- We feel confident that neither of us will ever become violent or bullying
- We don't threaten or call each other nasty names
- We generally finish important discussions without allowing interruptions, and without slamming doors, storming out, etc.
- We don't fear the process of working out disagreements
- We don't think of anger as destructive
- We know how to phrase our criticism and anger in productive ways
- We express "I love you" frequently, both verbally and non-verbally
- We don't bring up old hurts and irrelevancies when we disagree
- We don't believe that disagreement means failure

Let's look at how one couple used good communication skills to handle an extremely stressful experience of secret sharing. The following is part of a conversation between Letty and Al, both teachers in their early thirties. I had not seen them since the end of our successful marital counseling the previous summer.

Letty had called, saying she wanted to come in with Al to share something sensitive with him. She thought they could handle it alone, "But I don't want to take any chances," she said. To help you see how well they communicate, I've used brackets to highlight the clear messages within the conversation. You'll see how these clear messages made Letty's secret-sharing successful:

LETTY: I'm nervous about telling you this [here's how I feel], but I want to tell you because it's driving me crazy and making me feel distant from you [I want to be close to you, even while I feel upset]. As a child I was molested by Uncle Harvey for over a year. I'm sure this makes you angry [I'm sensitive to how you feel], but I don't want you to do anything crazy. I just want you to tell me everything's okay [here's what I want], and I want us to figure out how to deal with this [I think of us as a team].

AL: I'm totally stunned. How did this happen? How could you not tell me before now? I feel really insulted [here's how I feel]. Didn't you trust me all this time [I'd like more information]?

LETTY: I guess I understand how you would feel that way [you can express your feelings without me feeling attacked]. But I just couldn't tell you before. Now I can. I have changed, grown up some [I can handle your feelings without having to make you wrong]. I guess I've also gotten braver. And I believe in our marriage more [I can acknowledge loving you when things are rough].

An awkward silence filled the room, as husband and wife avoided each other's eyes. They each tried to speak once or twice, but choked back the words before they could come out. Finally, Al pounded his fist on the table. A few tears trickled down his cheek.

AL: I'm really sorry such a terrible thing happened to you [here's how I feel]. And I'm glad you feel better having told me [I'm pleased to help ease your pain, even while I'm upset myself]. But what am I supposed to do now? I'm totally humiliated. I've been relating to this damn guy for years, not knowing how he tried to ruin my wife's life. He must think I'm either a total wimp or a complete fool [I can express my anger without needing to destroy or discredit you].

LETTY: I don't think he does, but I can see how you might feel that way [I know that feelings can be more important than facts; I won't try to talk you out of your feelings]. When you're less upset we can talk about that more [We finish difficult discussions].

AL: Well, I'm going to get even with that lunatic.

LETTY: We need to talk about this a lot more before we do anything about it. I absolutely do not want you to go off and do anything in the heat of the moment [I expect your cooperation as my partner in dealing with this issue].

There was more silence, as the two of them struggled with their feelings. As Al's face grew darker, Letty became scared.

LETTY: I'd like us to hug so I know everything is okay [I want to be close even though we're in conflict].

AL: I'm not in the mood. I think I want to be left alone [Here's what I want].

LETTY: Will you at least tell me you love me [I'm willing to ask for what I want even when it's risky]?

AL: Yeah. Of course I love you. I'm just really upset. I'm sure I'll get over it . . . I don't know how, but I suppose I will [I'm willing to stay connected with you in a small way even when we're not fully connected].

LETTY: Can I do anything to help?

AL: Tell me you understand why I'm so upset [Here's what I need to feel closer].

Letty agreed, and the session proceeded. When it ended, Letty and Al decided they wanted to work on the issue themselves for a while. We agreed to meet again in two weeks.

I felt proud listening to the two of them handle Letty's secret. Their communication wasn't perfect, but it was obviously very effective. Letty and Al know how to handle problems as a team, rather than as opponents.

The relationship

In addition to good communication, other aspects of a strong relationship contribute to successful sharing. Here are some guidelines:

- We spend time together each week talking about things other than the kids and the household
- We are concerned about each other's happiness and pain
- We are each satisfied with the other's commitment to the relationship
- We respect each other's inner experience, even if we disagree with or don't understand it
- We love each other
- We like each other
- We each feel entitled to expect that a partner deal with difficult issues without too much withdrawing, whining, or punishing
- We both believe that our partnership is bigger than either person's temporary feelings
- We are each able to put ourselves in the other's place, and to consider what a particular event means to him or her, rather than only to ourselves
- We each believe that any pain the other causes is unintentional—at worst, thoughtless, rather than deliberate

You don't need every one of these to make sharing successful, but the more you have, the more likely it will be that sharing will produce the healthy results you want.

The individual

Perhaps the most important resource you can have for sharing sexual secrets productively is the sense of being okay. Or, as educator Gloria Blum puts it, "The ability and willingness to give yourself approval."

If you'll recall the Secrecy Imperative—"My sexuality and

I are bad, so I must hide both"—you can see that the sense of being okay makes secrecy seem far less urgent.

When you have high self-esteem, you are also less likely to blame others for your bad feelings. Thus, you would be less likely to use your secret as a weapon, which is a demeaning thing to do. Seeing yourself more as a partner rather than as an adversary or victim, you'd think of sharing as a relationship experience, not something you do to someone else. At the same time, you could more easily handle disagreement, realizing that love doesn't always require agreement.

Other personal resources that will help if you decide to share are intelligence, a sense of humor, the ability to tolerate stress, patience, and objectivity—all the wonderful attributes we wish we had. The whole thing reminds me of the man who spent his life looking for the perfect woman: "And when I finally found her," he said ruefully, "she was looking for the perfect man."

WARNING SIGNS

In some situations, of course, sharing is not appropriate. Relationships that lack the resources to handle the stress of serious sharing often have these symptoms:

- I'm definitely planning to leave the relationship
- My partner doesn't care about me
- I don't really care about my partner
- There is little or poor communication between us
- There is little trust between us
- My partner has proven he can't keep confidences
- My partner and I are very competitive with each other
- Our relationship seems to allow only one of us to be okay at a time
- My partner punishes me when he or she is upset
- I punish my partner when I'm upset

- My partner and I can't talk twenty minutes about anything important without fighting
- I can never predict how my partner will react to things
- My partner has said, "Don't tell me"
- Everybody has warned me against the sharing I'm considering
- There have been violent incidents or threats in the relationship

How does one deal with situations in which individuals lack resources? Productive sharing will be difficult or even impossible. What are the warning signs?

First, any form of low self-esteem. This includes constantly apologizing, thinking you're stupid, wishing you were someone else, not understanding why people spend time with you, and never expecting to get your way.

If these indicators of low self-esteem are present, however, you should only feel *warned* about sharing, rather than discouraged or dissuaded. After all, people with low self-esteem, and their relationships, benefit most from sharing. And, of course, sharing is a way to raise your self-esteem.

You should also feel warned if you lack the resources mentioned above; that is, intelligence, sense of humor, etc. These are some additional warning signs:

- You can't tolerate your partner being upset
- You're prone to feeling guilty about everything
- You're always angry
- You've been violent a few times
- You think you should run your relationship, because of your gender, age, intelligence, etc.
- You think relationships are overrated or a waste of time

If these personal or relational warning signs are familiar, what should you do? Most important, pay attention. Evaluate the message of these warning signs thoughtfully, instead of ignoring them or overreacting to them. Use your good judgment. That's the thing you gain from experience which, ironically, you gain from bad judgment.

In this chapter, you have examined your motives and resources for sharing. How does your situation look right now? If you feel very upset, make sure you have someone to talk to, whether it's your partner or someone else. You don't need to talk about any particular secret, just the fact that you're upset.

In an ideal situation, the relationship can handle a partner sharing. He or she is sharing for good reasons and feels sex is wholesome and acceptable.

Only you can decide when sharing is appropriate in your life. Experience is a valuable aid in making your choice. Experience . . . that's what enables us to recognize a mistake when we've made it once again.

What circumstances are best for sharing? That's covered in the next chapter.

THINK ABOUT IT

As I consider sharing, do I have any of these good reasons?

☐ Getting closer to my partner
☐ Improving our sexual relationship
☐ Increasing my self-esteem
☐ Reducing the physical or emotional stresses of secrecy
☐ Changing a relationship, or supporting a current change

As I consider sharing, do I have any of these bad reasons?

☐ Getting revenge
☐ Punishing or humiliating someone
☐ Relieving a heavy burden of guilt
☐ Inviting criticism or punishment
☐ Testing a relationship
☐ Creating a smokescreen

As I consider sharing, which of the following resources can I depend on?

☐ Good communication skills
☐ A good communication system
☐ A solid relationship
☐ A sense that I'm okay
☐ A sense of humor
☐ The ability to handle stress
☐ My own patience and objectivity

9

PREPARING
FOR
SHARING

So, you've decided to share a sexual secret. Assuming it's for the good reasons we've discussed, congratulations!

You probably feel both excited and nervous. Maybe you're also getting ready to be embarrassed, ashamed, or angry. All of these feelings are normal.

This chapter discusses how to prepare for sharing. Ideally, you'll feel good about yourself before sharing, and you'll feel free to articulate your feelings and needs clearly. You'll have the sense that your relationship is a cooperative partnership. And you'll arrange the kind of pragmatic support that you need, such as privacy, confidentiality, or a friendly backrub halfway through.

There are four primary ways of preparing for sharing:

- Preparing yourself
- Preparing your partner and relationship

- Preparing the circumstances
- Preparing for the consequences

Let's examine them one at a time.

PREPARING YOURSELF

The most important part of preparing for sharing is self-preparation. You, after all, are the one who will set the tone for the sharing event, provide the agenda, and guide the interaction.

Being prepared means being aware of your resources, so you can use them most effectively. In this section we will look at the various forms these resources take.

Steps 1 to 7 are, in a way, review steps. They help you recall useful information you already know, and bring together seemingly unrelated facts in helpful ways. These steps will help you transform your feelings and thoughts into resources.

Step 8, visualization, synthesizes all the steps before it. It guides you to rehearse mentally the outcomes that you hope to accomplish by sharing.

Together, the eight steps that follow are meant to give you a sense of *entitlement*. This is the sense that your needs are basically reasonable, and that your emotional reality deserves to be recognized. You don't have to earn this entitlement by being "right." Every human is born with it, including you. Why? Simply because you are okay. Not perfect—just perfectly adequate.

Being aware of your entitlement is an important aspect of preparing for sharing because it supports the loving, enlightened part of you. When a sharing interaction gets difficult, a sense of entitlement also helps you keep from getting defensive. It helps you to feel close to your partner, rather than seeing him or her as an adversary.

As you look at each of these eight steps, see how each

one relates to you. In fact, you will probably find it valuable to keep some notes on how you can apply each one to the sharing you're planning to do.

1. Clarifying goals

We begin Chapter 9 as we began Chapter 8—by examining and clarifying the goals of sharing. When you feel confident of your goals, you can fall back on them as a resource when you are confused, tongue-tied, or feeling guilty.

Elaine, for example, has a common enough secret: she wants to make love more often. Because her husband, Ned, has for years been considered the sex expert of the couple, Elaine hadn't even thought to assert her own needs. Instead, she silently harbored her secret.

Elaine's therapy focused on giving herself permission; specifically, making it okay to want what she wanted. Typically, Elaine judged her own needs using others' standards. She often feared that these standards showed that her desires were wrong.

During the course of therapy, Elaine decided to share the true level of her sexual interest. Her goals were to improve her sex life and to start asserting herself more as an equal partner with Ned. I supported the sharing she planned.

Elaine prepared for weeks before sharing. The sharing itself was a difficult experience. As she told me afterward, "I got nervous and flustered when I told him, just as I feared. Ned wasn't openly angry, but he wasn't cooperative either. 'This is too hard,' I thought. 'Maybe I should just stop.'

"But I recalled what we'd discussed in session," she continued, a smile softening her face. "I remembered the goals I wrote down, the sense of direction I felt. I remembered how we had agreed that my goals were okay, even loving, and that I had no wish to hurt or insult Ned.

"So I took a deep breath, and plunged ahead. Ned was surprised and a little taken aback, I know. But we kept talking. We seem to be working things out." When Elaine began to falter in the thin air of relationship confrontation, clear goals were like extra oxygen that gave her a second wind.

Elaine's experience shows how important it is to review your goals and motives prior to sharing. Use the material in Chapter 8, recalling what you learned about yourself. If your approach seemed positive a chapter ago, it's still positive now. If not, it isn't too late to reformulate or postpone your plans for sharing.

2. Assessing and strengthening your support network

No healthy person is completely self sufficient. We need others to support our risks and decisions, to celebrate our victories, and to sympathize with our frustrations and despair. As you deal with the stress of preparing to share, and later with sharing's consequences, you will appreciate the caring of others.

A support network consists of one or more people whom you can trust to help you through self-doubt or pain. This group may include a close friend, minister, therapist, sister, even an entire sewing circle.

When you share a sexual secret, it is often with the person whose support you normally count on the most. If he or she is upset, that support may be least available exactly when you need it the most.

So instead of depending solely on your mate's support, consider friends, family, and co-workers. If you wish, sound them out first on a smaller issue to gauge their reaction. You may be surprised to discover who is eager to support you. If appropriate, consider seeing a professional such as a clergy member or therapist.

Books can also offer support, particularly if you feel alone or a little crazy. Some helpful ones include *Women Who Love Too Much, Necessary Losses, It Will Never Happen to Me, The Hite Report, Why Men Are the Way They Are, When Living Hurts,* and *Night Thoughts.*

As you think about sharing your secret, ask yourself what

kind of emotional support is available. Make certain that the kind of support you would most like to have is available.

3. Clarifying your vision of sexuality

Most of us never sit down and articulate our thoughts about sexuality. And yet we all have sexual convictions, feelings, and intuitions.

With the Secrecy Imperative as our heritage, sexual negativity is virtually unavoidable. While it is sometimes blatant ("Fornication is a sin"), it is often subtle (magazines accepting ads for harmful douches but not for pleasurable vibrators).

A coherent vision of sexuality is a valuable asset when you share a secret. If you view sex as wholesome, moral, and life-affirming, your beliefs can serve as guideposts while you share. Just as a boat is aided by sailing toward a landmark or buoy, your vision can help keep you from being blown off course by having your words or intentions turned against you.

A story from my own life illustrates this. The son of a friend called one day and asked to meet with me. I had watched this young man grow up over the years, and I liked him. He was now a well-known freshman athlete at a big university, home for winter break. He sounded troubled.

It wasn't a therapy session, so I invited him to my house. He declined a Pepsi when he arrived, eager to talk right away. "It's the locker room," he said simply. "It's a big club, and I don't belong." I asked him to tell me more.

"The only thing the guys ever talk about is girls," he continued. "Fine. I love talking about girls. But everyone talks about what they do with them. And because I'm a star on the field . . ." he hesitated.

"They figure you're a star off the field, too?" I suggested.

Ken was relieved. "Yeah, that's it," he said. "They want to know who I sleep with, and when, and how much, and all that. But I don't . . . I haven't . . . I never . . ."

This was obviously hard for him. "Ken, lots of kids are virgins when they enter college," I said. "Many even graduate that way. There's nothing wrong with you, if that's what you're worried about."

He relaxed a bit. "Well, that's half of it," he said. "The other half is what do I say? Should I pretend? Should I tell people to shut up? I feel really alone with this."

Feeling alone in a roomful of peers and admirers is a sad experience. "You're a big hero at school, bright and well-liked," I said. "So obviously, you've *chosen* not to have intercourse. Aside from all the pressure, do you feel okay about your choice? Does it feel like what's best for you? Remember, you don't need to apologize, or to talk with anyone about it against your will. If a choice works for you, there's no reason to change it."

I paused and let this sink in.

"But it sure sounds like you'd appreciate sharing your dilemma with someone," I continued gently. Ken needed to feel normal, and he needed a way to cope with the pressure. "Is there a guy on the team you can trust?" I asked. "Maybe he could help you change the subject when it comes up, or deflect some of the attention. At the very least, maybe you could feel like yourself with him."

The idea delighted Ken as he started to focus on the positive aspect of his decision instead of the criticism in his teammates' jokes. When he used his own view of sexuality as a compass, Ken felt better about himself, and he could see how sharing made sense. With the energy of youth, he began to plan his personal strategy immediately.

When I next saw him, during spring break, he seemed happier, more satisfied with himself. He had talked to a few teammates, and found out they were uncomfortable, too. He felt less isolated and was trusting his own judgment more. "Once you realize your decision is right for you," he told me, "handling other people is easy, isn't it?"

In fact, some of Ken's maturity seems to be rubbing off

on the rest of the team. He says they don't pressure each other about sex nearly as much as they used to.

4. Clarifying your vision of the relationship

Stop now and remind yourself of the kind of relationship you desire. Take the luxury of daydreaming for a moment, as you create a mental image of what you'd have if your relationship were exactly as you'd like.

Now focus on how your secret, when shared, could be part of this sound relationship. If your partner is frightened or angered by your sharing, he or she may say your behavior has threatened the relationship. Don't get drawn into defending yourself, which often leads to unpleasant or destructive fighting.

Instead, *you* set the terms for any conflict that arises from your sharing. Use your relationship vision to navigate the sharing experience, inviting your partner to talk about his or her vision as well.

As you consider the relationship you want to create, think about these issues:

- What kind of relationship rights and power do you want each of you to have?
- What kinds of roles do you want each of you to play?
- How do you want to divide household and other responsibilities?
- How much and what kind of communication do you want?
- How much routine sharing and contact do you want?

Let's look at how a relationship vision would be used during secret-sharing.

Carlos was a successful carpenter who had never been married. Sexually active with several women in nearby towns, he "just knew I wasn't the father type. Being an uncle is perfect for me." On his thirtieth birthday he decided to get a vasectomy at the local Planned Parenthood clinic.

Four months later, Carlos's family gathered at his parents' home for Thanksgiving. The next morning, he asked his mother and father if they could sit and talk.

"I know you're very eager for me to raise a family," he said, "so I thought I should tell you. I'm not going to have children. I've been to a doctor and had a vasectomy. I know it's not what you wanted, but I hope you'll accept it."

After a stunned silence, Carlos's parents said everything he was afraid they would. "You're so selfish," cried his mother. "How could you run off and do such an impulsive thing?" "You'll regret being so arrogant!" his enraged father shouted. "You'll wish you hadn't thought you could predict the future. Besides, how dare you do this without talking to us first?"

Carlos, of course, felt terrible. Like virtually all men who have vasectomies, he was thrilled with his. He hadn't had a single regret—until now. Now Carlos wanted to defend himself, apologize, plead for understanding. He felt guilty and hurt.

But, as Carlos tells the story, "Then I thought, wait a minute, this makes no sense. How could this have gone from right to wrong overnight?" Carlos took a deep breath and looked directly at his parents. "Listen," he interrupted. "Listen to this so-called conversation. You say you're angry that I didn't talk to you, but here I am talking, and you're going crazy.

"All you've done so far is tell me how stupid my decision is," he said. "You haven't asked me why I did it, what it was like, how I feel about the results, nothing." His voice shook with emotion. "You're hurt and angry? Well, I'm hurt and angry."

The room was suddenly quiet. "You two are very special to me," Carlos finally said. "I want to have a special relationship with you. But . . ." Carlos paused, as unhappy with the truth as he knew his parents were. "But we still have a long way to go."

I think Carlos handled this situation pretty well. His mom

and dad were ready to have a big fight about how wrong he was. Carlos, however, refused to get into a "bad child–angry parent" argument. He stuck to his vision of the relationship he wanted with them, communicating as directly—and lovingly—as he could.

His folks will never be thrilled with his decision, but they are making progress toward resuming the satisfying relationship with Carlos that they used to enjoy so much. They notice and appreciate the way he loves his nieces, for example. And they're delighted with his latest gift—enlargements of some photos he took of the girls during the family's Christmas gathering.

5. Evaluating and accepting your feelings

Knowledge, we know, is power. We generally don't apply this idea to our feelings, but when sharing a secret, the more you understand your feelings, the more you can steer the interaction toward your goals.

In our noisy, fast-paced world, it can be hard to know how you feel. Our body will tell us, if we listen: the insomnia, tight throat, pounding head, damp hands, knotted stomach, and lost (or insatiable) appetite are clear signals, *if we look and listen.* Other ways to discover our feelings include writing in a diary, going for a quiet walk, and watching the way others react to us.

Everyone preparing to share a secret experiences certain feelings, usually uncomfortable ones. Rather than ignoring or denying them, you are better off focusing on them. You then have a good chance of accepting and dealing with them directly.

Here are some feelings you might have:

- Fear: I'll be judged; I'll be rejected; I'll damage my relationship.
- Guilt: I've done bad things; I'm bad; I've misled my partner.

- Anger: I can't believe I've had to hide things for so long; how dare you judge me.
- Self-criticism: I can't believe I was willing to lie; I'm disappointed to realize I am so insecure; I have lied to myself.

You may also have a sense of power or pride about taking a risk, asserting your needs, stopping the lies, and restoring your integrity. The combination of guilt and pride can be confusing, but it's a normal response to emotional growth.

What does it mean to deal with your feelings? Partly, it means *stopping for a moment and experiencing your insides.* If there's hurt in there, you need to *feel* hurt. When you really feel hurt (or anxious, angry, or sad), you don't want to continue with business as usual.

We all need to express how we feel. And the way the human brain is built, if we don't do it directly—by words, tears, or physical action—inevitably, we'll do it indirectly—by accidents, alcohol abuse, lowered sex drive, senseless fighting, or covertly sabotaging a partner.

The first step toward expressing your feelings is accepting them. Do not confuse this with liking or even approving of your feelings. You are simply accepting your inner reality, accepting what *is*.

An inner voice might describe the acceptance of feelings in one of these ways:

- "It's okay to feel like this."
- "I know this feeling is temporary."
- "I am bigger than this particular feeling."
- "I have felt this way before, and gone on."
- "Other reasonable people feel this way."
- "This feeling is part of who I am."
- "This feeling doesn't negate any other parts of me."

Accepting your feelings is accepting yourself. It helps you stay true to your goals. It helps you get through your pain, and it keeps you from assuming that just because you're uncomfortable, you're doing something wrong. When you're growing, in fact, the opposite is more often true.

6. Be sensitive to yourself

When preparing to share a secret, consider your own needs and moods as well as your partner's. Respect yourself.

We've talked about relaxing, feeling supported, and being clear about your goals. Here is how some people I know have made their sharing experiences more satisfying:

- "My husband often accuses me of being undersexed, so I took a hot bath right before sharing to feel sexier."
- "I was so nervous that I wasn't even sure I would go through with it, so I planned our conversation for right after jogging, when I usually feel strong."
- "I was concerned about becoming bitchy about the whole thing. So to help me keep a positive attitude, I decided to share on our anniversary, when I knew I'd be feeling close to him."

What can you do to personalize your own sharing?

7. Transforming the fear of rejection

Certain human fears are universal: these include fear of the dark, of ageing, of the unknown, and of death. And there is fear of rejection. At no time is this fear greater than when you think about sharing a secret.

We have already talked about the source and expression of this fear several times. Let us look at it again in yet another way: as a source of energy to be transformed and used.

To do so we have to look beneath the surface, asking what lies closest to the fear of rejection. The answer is threefold: First, our desire for closeness and connection. Second, our idealization of another person. (If not for these, rejection would not pose such a profound threat.) Third is self-criticism—our sense of deserving rejection, on some level, fuels our fear that it will happen.

Whether they make sense or not, these primitive emotions drive our fear—unless we deal with them consciously. So you must interrupt your fear, getting to the feelings under it. Then you can remind yourself of your good intentions, to feel close; of your highest aspirations, your idealizations of your partner; and of your reflexive negativity—your self-criticism.

If you do this, you will short-circuit your own fear. You'll soon start noticing how much less you say, "I can't help it; I just feel afraid."

One way to be aware of your emotions is by examining your assumptions about the sharing interaction. What do you suppose will happen? How do you imagine your partner will feel? How will he or she respond to you? How will you handle that response? What will be the long-term results? Does this feel like a painful situation you've been in before? Do you think things will unfold this time as they did then?

If we were like "Star Trek's" Mr. Spock, we would anticipate the future using accurate data and perfect logic. Instead, our judgment is normally colored by simple human fears and desires. You can prepare for sharing by examining your assumptions about yourself and your partner.

Then take a Mr. Spock-like attitude: How likely is it, *really,* that my husband will yell at me, that I will fall apart when he yells, that he will leave me when I do? Or, how likely is it, *really,* that my adult daughter will tell me she's disgusted, refusing to meet my new lover? Lay out your own worst scenarios and evaluate their likelihood. You'll almost certainly find that the facts suggest a milder outcome than you fear.

The other way to handle your fears is to discuss them. Tell your partner that you fear rejection, explaining what lies behind that for you. Talking about your desire for closeness and your fear of losing it can be one of the most intimate moments in any relationship. Emotional energy is powerful; use it consciously. Instead of letting it isolate you through fear, use it to create connection.

Reinforcing your relationship by talking about your fear sets the stage for sharing secrets more effectively.

8. Rehearsing and visualizing sharing

Bernie Zilbergeld writes in *Mind Power* (1987) that positive mental rehearsal can improve performance in virtually all of life's tasks. World-class athletes have been "visualizing" for years now, with startling results. You can, too.

The first stage is to practice being relaxed. To start, just breathe a little slower and deeper. Drop your shoulders and let your jaw go slack. Feel the warm sense of well-being this produces in your body.

Incredible! You can create this relaxed sensation at will under any circumstance, simply by choosing to. Resolve now that you'll remember to do it as you begin to share, and again while you share.

Now close your eyes. Imagine telling your partner your secret, and notice how you're maintaining your composure under stress. You're breathing, even smiling occasionally, feeling confident and focused on your goals. Visit this fantasy for thirty seconds each day before you share. That is the reality you'll create.

Now that you've rehearsed mentally, do it physically. You may feel silly at first, but this step really does help. Imagine you're with the person you'll be speaking with. Begin your conversation out loud. Speak a few words you're likely to say then, like "Doris, this is awkward for me, but I really want to share what's on my mind." Or "Bob, I want to tell you something that will probably surprise you. I'd like you to just listen until I'm finished."

Note your tone of voice, manner of standing or sitting, and other forms of presentation. Start speaking out loud again, adjusting your style to reflect better your intentions. Want to be more assertive? Rehearse speaking that way, as if you already are assertive. Practice and repetition will help make it so.

Finally, visualize—mentally rehearse—getting the results you want from your sharing. This may include being understood in a new way, negotiating specific relationship changes, having a deeper sense of closeness with the other person, or feeling proud of yourself.

If the image doesn't come easily, take a deep breath and stay with it. Above all, if you can only visualize a result of problems and drama, take some time to imagine an alternate, positive ending. Sharing may not be as much of a mess as you fear. Don't be one of those people who can't take *yes* for an answer.

PREPARING YOUR PARTNER AND YOUR RELATIONSHIP

The amount that you need to prepare your partner and relationship for sharing depends on the nature of your secret. In some situations such preparation may be unnecessary, while in others, weeks or months of preparation may be appropriate.

The goal of this section is to assist you in 1) recalling and reaffirming the special bond, history, and resources you and your partner have; and 2) thinking of yourselves as a problem-solving *team,* rather than as individuals with competing interests.

When two people have these two points in mind, sharing has a much better chance of bringing positive results.

Start by asking yourself what typically nurtures your relationship. It may be a walk in the park, a half-hour with a photo album, reading together in bed, or something else. Just thinking about this will be instructive. So will discussing it with your partner. You'll be looking at the nuts and bolts of intimacy.

Do some of these activities prior to sharing. It will help create a warm, healing atmosphere.

Next, look at and clean up the communication in your relationship. Discuss the non-verbal ways you two "talk" to each other, along with what they usually mean. Here are some examples, with interpretations of what they commonly imply.

BEHAVIOR	TYPICAL MEANING
Patting someone on the head	Dismissing what the person says
Busying yourself with chores	Not wanting to support an idea, but wanting to avoid a confrontation during a conversation
Reading the newspaper while listening to someone speak	Maintaining distance, expressing a lack of interest
Stroking someone seductively while he or she speaks	Wanting to avoid a serious conversation, or trying to get permission or to manipulate someone
Breaking matchsticks or tearing little bits of paper	Feeling restless, resentful, anxious

Partners rarely discuss their non-verbal communication. Instead, most of us assume that we know what these gestures mean—although doubt may nag at us from time to time. To help make your sharing more effective, explore the non-verbal communication in your relationship. Start by talking about a misunderstanding you once had, or a question you have now.

Similarly, attend to the verbal component of your relationship. While all of us like to think that we understand each other's words, this isn't always true. Lewis Carroll put it this way in *Through the Looking Glass:*

"When *I* use a word," Humpty Dumpty said, "it means just what I choose it to mean—neither more nor less." "The question is," said Alice, "whether you *can* make words mean so many different things." "The question is," replied Humpty, "which is to be master—that is all."

Do you generally feel understood by your partner? If not, discuss this with him or her. Your goal is not to decide whom to blame, but rather to explore how you feel, what the results are, and how to improve this outcome. Only then can you begin to change the communication system.

For example, do one or both of you interrupt frequently? Do you feel you don't always get your turn? Do you wish your partner gave you more feedback? Perhaps you desire a different kind of response. Instead of empathizing with you, for example, many people try to fix your feelings. They may try to convince you there's no reason to be upset, tell you it doesn't look good to cry in public, try to solve a problem before you're ready, and so on.

Do either of you use particular words or expressions that always irritate the other? Some parents are always nagging a child about not living up to his "potential." Or tell a teenager that she's not "tolerant" of others. Some wives criticize their husbands' lack of "manliness," while many men complain that their wives are "too emotional."

When particular words get a negative history between two people, they disrupt and eventually prevent productive communication. Take a moment to list a few such words in your relationship. Share the list with your partner, who may want to add a few. Agree to use different, neutral terms whenever possible.

Here are some examples of "loaded" terms from my patients' lives:

- Tolerant
- Selfish
- Mama's boy
- A real man
- A real wife

- A little more patience
- Try harder
- A real killjoy
- A stick-in-the-mud
- Be cooperative

Different terms, of course, are sensitive for different people.

The next step in preparing your partner for sharing is to assure him or her of your commitment. Tell your partner explicitly that your intention is to communicate, not to criticize or punish. Let him or her know that you care about the feelings your sharing will kindle in him or her: "Jim, this will be hard for me, so I imagine it will be hard for you. I promise to listen to everything you have to say about it—I really want to know what you think." This can help your partner avoid feeling like your adversary.

Most people have anxiety about this process, and sharing it with your partner is always appropriate. It activates your partner's natural concern for you, and also helps him or her know that you're not just coldly plowing ahead without concern. Keep in mind, as we have noted before, that talking about your anxiety tends to reduce it.

How do you and your partner handle stress? Here are some common answers people give:

- "I just try to ignore it, pretend it's not there."
- "We make love."
- "We bring up old arguments."
- "I eat, usually stuff I shouldn't."
- "I go and spend money." (Some people call this Retail Therapy.)
- "We focus on the kids, either positively or negatively."
- "We watch TV as a way of taking a time out from each other."
- "One or both of us has a drink."
- "We invite other people over, and relate to them."

- "We do a few chores, or catch up on some office work."
- "I go to a department store." (When the going gets tough, the tough go shopping.)

Since you probably haven't given the subject much thought, do so now, because sharing your secret will probably create stress. What are the results of the ways you handle stress? Do they make the problem worse? Do they reinforce a feeling of powerlessness? Do they make the return of stress inevitable?

What better ways can you think of to handle relationship stress? You may find it helpful to ask your partner (spouse, child, colleague) to brainstorm with you. One way to do this is to recall, together, times when you handled difficult situations as a team. You might have talked long into the night several times a week, or spent a day at the beach thinking about things, or even bought a book or consulted an expert.

Most relationships have at least a few successful experiences, even if they happened many years ago. You each felt heard then, didn't you? And you felt like partners, right? Remembering this feeling is the first step toward recreating it.

When you've come this far, you have prepared your partner and your relationship. Love, in some form, should be in the air. Your team's resources should be familiar and easily accessible. Sharing is becoming a greater possibility every moment.

To reward yourself for working so hard, go for another walk in the park. There's more work to do when you return.

PREPARING THE MOMENT AND THE CIRCUMSTANCES

Flowers and candlelight? Franks and beans? Whips and chains? Preparing the setting and choosing the moment for sharing can be tricky.

Clearly, a receptive mood and feeling of cooperation are what you want most. There are ways to make that more likely, but you need to be realistic. You won't always get that, even if you do everything right. Don't take it personally, and don't let it stop you from sharing.

Some say there is nothing for a case of nerves like a case of beer. But sharing secrets demands clear thinking and sincere feeling, both of which alcohol inhibits. So don't choose a time when you know that either of you will have been drinking.

That might eliminate Sunday afternoon during football season, or midnight after guests go home from your dinner party. Even if you are feeling close to each other at these times, alcohol may make the sharing frustrating or even ugly.

If you can't find a time when both of you are sober *and* willing to spend time together just talking, your relationship is in serious trouble.

You should also avoid sharing when there is unresolved anger or similar feelings between you and your partner. In such a situation, sharing is frequently interpreted as part of the unfinished emotional business. It may even be seen as punishment. A partner may think you're saying, "Since you refuse to stop flirting at parties [which we argued about yesterday], I'm revealing my dissatisfaction with our lovemaking [to hurt you]."

Here are some examples of strong feelings which, if currently on the table, may complicate sharing:

- "You still haven't done that chore you promised you'd do."
- "Sex has been lousy (or lacking) lately."
- "When will your brother ever leave?"
- "I can't believe you spent so much money on that."
- "When are you gonna make that kid behave?"
- "You embarrassed me again last night."

- "I'm nervous about the amount of time you spend at the track."
- "I wish you would go to the doctor about that pain."

These are important feelings in the life of a relationship. You already know you shouldn't ignore them. Similarly, don't discount their significance by clouding the air with the feelings generated by sharing.

So what should you look for?

Time. Time to present your feelings, hear your partner's response, and discuss the implications. And two more things: time to process the event itself, and to reconnect afterward. That might not happen the same day, so be open to making time for more talk later in the week.

Before you share, get your partner's agreement for a long talk. If he or she is unable or unwilling to have a long talk now, ask when that will be possible. Don't complain, just request information. Every relationship needs to have a neutral, agreed-upon way of one partner asking the other, "Okay, if not now, when?"

Time's complement is privacy. In order to make sharing the loving, satisfying experience you desire, you need privacy from others, and freedom from distraction. That means not answering the phone, not basting the roast, not moving the garden hose, not checking on the wash. Don't start activities that require this kind of attention when you plan to share. And don't begin to share if you have already started these kinds of activities.

Finally, make sure you have the appropriate level of confidentiality. Although this may seem obvious, consider the result of not making your wishes absolutely clear.

Listen, for instance, to one woman tell her story. Anna was 45, the wife of a Navy officer, when I met her.

"I was raped about a year go, right on the base," she told me. "It turned our lives upside down. I guess I was in shock for a long time. And my nose was broken, so I looked awful for months, too. At first, we told the kids I had had an accident," she said. Such deception isn't unusual. It's a way of denying a terrible experience, as well as an attempt to spare loved ones pain, guilt, and shame.

"Well, the lie worked for a while," Anna continued, "although with periodic calls from the police and me bursting into tears unpredictably, the story was stretching thinner and thinner. Finally, encouraged by the social worker at the base, Jorge and I decided to share the secret with our two kids. They were six and ten at the time.

"Well, just explaining about rape was terribly draining. I'm still not sure they totally understood what I said. But it made me feel better," Anna said, "somehow cleaner, as if I wasn't carrying around that little part of the rape anymore."

So far, so good. The problem came a week later, when a friend of Anna's six-year-old daughter Jenny asked her about the rape. "I just about flipped," she says. "It turns out Jenny and her friends were talking about their mothers one day, and Jenny told the other kids what had happened."

That was bad enough. "But that same week, the mother of a neighborhood kid called and yelled at me to keep my problems to myself. When I asked what she meant, she referred to my 'damn rape.' She said the story had practically paralyzed her eleven-year-old daughter with fright.

"When I told my ten year old the story that night, she started to cry. 'I was so sad for you,' she said between sobs, 'and I didn't know what to do. Finally my friend Lois asked me what was wrong, and I told her. Now you're mad at me.'

"I was mad, mad at both of them," said Anna, "but I realize it was my fault, too. I should've really stressed that this was a private event in our family, and made much more time for all of us to talk about it further."

Anna and Jorge would have been more satisfied with the outcome of their sharing if they had been more sensitive to the needs and feelings of their children. Such sensitivity is important in preparing any moment for telling a secret.

You can probably name several times during a typical week when your partner is more relaxed than usual. In our household, these include Sunday brunch; after picking fruit from the trees in our yard; and after an evening bath. Take a moment now to think about such receptive moments in your home.

But don't get hung up on preparing the perfect moment. There is no such thing; besides, your concern may simply reflect the very problem you're trying to solve: one more time that you're trying to make things perfect for your partner; one more time that you feel your truth must be packaged in an "acceptable" way.

PREPARING FOR THE CONSEQUENCES

Just as consequences complete a sharing experience, preparing for consequences completes the preparation for sharing. There's a nice symmetry to it.

Nearly everyone who shares a secret fears the consequences of their actions. While we don't know what sharing's ultimate impact will be, we fear the permanence of the results. And most of us assume the consequences will be painful, for ourselves and for our partners.

Unconsciously, I think we also fear that our sharing will invite our partner's sharing. What if he or she says something we don't want to hear?

To prepare for sharing, acknowledge such fears. Admit to yourself, right out loud, your vision of the worst possible consequences, along with the less drastic, but more likely ones. Some common consequences that people fear are:

• My partner will reject me
• My partner will share a secret that will greatly hurt me

- My partner won't take me seriously
- My partner will punish me
- My partner will break my confidentiality
- I will realize we've got serious trouble
- I will cause problems for other people
- I will regret sharing

Interestingly, few people acknowledge their fear of positive outcomes, such as:

- My partner will desire change as much as I do
- My partner will encourage me to share more
- I will discover that my partner understands me better than I thought
- I will discover that my relationship is stronger than I thought

The irony is that any of these can be as scary as the more negative results, because only one thing is as frightening as isolation—increased contact. That's why we are uncomfortable when people stare at us or when our eyes meet a stranger's in an elevator. It also explains why people sometimes argue after their most intimate times together.

In addition to confronting your fears, another way to prepare is to ask yourself, "Whose problem would this particular consequence be?" The answer is not always "Mine."

Some, of course, *are* clearly yours. For example, you reveal that you used to play bondage games with your ex-husband, and your present lover decides he doesn't want to play them with you anymore. The thought that you've been intimate in this way with someone else ruins it for him. That's sad, but you'll have to accept it, at least for now.

On the other hand, some problems belong to the person with whom you have shared your secret. For example, you reveal that your sex drive is higher than your husband had thought, so now he feels jealous when you're in public. Assuming that you're not doing anything special to trigger those feelings in him, this is something that *he* must deal with.

Some consequences accrue to neither you nor your partner, but to the relationship.

Consider Faith and Johann, who came to see me because of his ejaculation difficulties. Johann could climax when stimulated by Faith's mouth or hand, but he couldn't ejaculate into Faith's vagina. What brought them into counseling, they said, was their desire to have a child in the next year or two. "We want to start getting ready now," Faith said warmly.

I usually see each partner individually at the start of couples counseling. In our private session, I asked Faith if she didn't mind the way they had sex. "Not at all," she replied quickly. "Johann is attentive and loving, and I usually have a good orgasm manually or orally." I asked the question one or two other ways, and I got the same answer. Accepting it for the time being, I moved on.

When the three of us assembled for the next couples session, the talk turned to sexual satisfaction. Faith looked at me. "You didn't really believe I was okay with our sex life, did you?" She was right; I hadn't felt her answer was complete.

"Why did I answer so quickly?" asked Faith rhetorically. "I'm so afraid of rocking the boat, of upsetting people. The truth is, I *do* mind our sex life. I resent watching you ejaculate, Johann, and feeling left out of it. I want a baby some day, sure, but I want this changed now. For *me*."

The secret was out. Johann, always the cool research scientist, remained detached. "How sad for you," he said quietly. "I hope you become less unhappy." In the weeks that followed, though, Faith become more unhappy. The reason was simple: Johann stopped making love with her. "I'm not in the mood lately," he said flatly. "Besides, I don't want Faith judging our sex life every time we do it."

It looked like a standoff. Faith felt guilty and angry, reinforced by Johann's self-righteousness. How long would it last? "No one can predict the future," observed the scientist. "That's right, Johann," I replied. "Right, but irrelevant.

"What's relevant," I continued, having gotten his attention, "is that you two have lost one of your forms of intimacy. I don't think that's merely Faith's problem. I think it's your marriage's problem. I'd like to know what your team is planning to do about it. And, if your team is not addressing the issue, why it isn't."

This, then, became the focus of the session. What did couplehood mean to these two people? How were they to deal with their mixed feelings about attachment and dependence? These questions, I felt, were central to resolving the symptom they came in with. Once Faith stopped pretending that everything was fine, changes in the relationship were inevitable.

Was Johann willing for their lives to become more intertwined? To his credit, he grudgingly agreed to explore the concept further, making it a central theme of our couples therapy. That was the beginning of each one's sense that they had a joint sexual relationship, something that went beyond their individual selves. That valuable perspective has stayed with Johann and Faith to this day.

But what if your partner rejects you? First, make sure that your feeling is accurate. Are you really being rejected? True rejection often sounds like this:

- "You don't really feel that way."
- "I have no time for that sort of crap."
- "I've heard this before, and I'm not interested."
- "If you were a real man/woman, you'd have worked that out by now."
- "If you're going to start complaining, I have plenty of my own complaints, so let's drop the whole thing."
- "You've got it all wrong."
- "If that's the way you feel, maybe you'd be happier with someone else."

If your partner responds to your sharing with this kind of attitude, let him or her know that you feel unheard and rejected. Suggest that you begin the conversation again, and describe your feelings and secret differently. Your partner's perspective and response may change as a result.

If your partner feels justified in rejecting you, you may want to try one or more of the following approaches:

- Ask what you can do to make yourself clearer
- Recall and remind your partner why you shared this
- Demand that your partner continue discussing this with you
- Suggest a discussion of the meaning of love and commitment in this relationship
- Take a break from the discussion, and come back again later
- Reassess your expectations about your sharing
- Reassess the relationship

What can help you pursue these responses? Patience and objectivity are valuable resources in coping with rejection. They help you remember that being connected to someone over time sometimes requires sitting out a short period of isolation and pain. They also help you see that you are sometimes the target for someone else's painful feelings.

While successful sharing requires sensitivity to your partner's needs, keep in mind that it's okay if he or she is upset about the sharing.

And, as we discussed, take advantage of your support network. Without invading your partner's privacy, share your concerns and feelings with those who understand you. Find out how others have dealt with similar situations. Allow them to remind you that you're terrific.

Finally, a sense of humor is invaluable. This is, according to Steve Martin, "The art of making people laugh without making them puke." Or, I might add, making them feel angry or demeaned. Gentle, affectionate humor helps you remind yourself and your partner that your relationship is bigger than whatever is happening at the moment. What a nice gift to give yourself and a loved one.

As you think about the issue of consequences, you may find your decision to share your secret wavering. Stay with that feeling of caution and reluctance. Sharing might not be appropriate after all, or maybe not with this person. There are some situations better handled through other parts of your support network rather than with your mate.

Perhaps you need more time. Take a walk through the next chapter, and imagine what life would be like and how you would feel—if you decide *not* to share.

THINK ABOUT IT

As I prepare to share, I have done the following:

- [ ] Clarified my goals
- [ ] Assessed and strengthened (if necessary) my support network
- [ ] Clarified my vision of sexuality
- [ ] Clarified my vision of the relationship
- [ ] Evaluated and accepted my feelings, needs, and moods
- [ ] Examined and worked on my fear of rejection
- [ ] Rehearsed and visualized sharing
- [ ] Acknowledged my fears
- [ ] Thought about whose problem the anticipated consequences will be
- [ ] Thought about the consequences of *not* sharing

As I prepare to share, I think about doing the following:

- [ ] Whatever activities commonly nurture my relationship
- [ ] Cleaning up the communication in my relationship (both verbal and nonverbal)
- [ ] Assuring my partner of my commitment to the relationship
- [ ] Preparing to handle the stress of sharing

As I prepare to share, I think about choosing the following circumstances:

- [ ] Neither of us has been drinking
- [ ] There are no unresolved bad feelings between us
- [ ] We have enough time to explore and handle the situation
- [ ] We have enough privacy
- [ ] We have the right amount of confidentiality

10

IF YOU
DECIDE NOT
TO SHARE

No man is lonely while eating spaghetti.
—ROBERT MORLEY

You haven't failed.

You're not bad or emotionally inhibited.

You've simply decided not to share one or more sexual secrets.

You're not alone.

After all, most people keep sexual secrets. Your secrecy, however, is now the result of conscious choice, not of feeling powerless.

Your understanding gives you a great advantage. True, your behavior may not look any different than it did before your decision. But now, after careful thought, you've *chosen* your behavior. Because you've taken charge of your own life, you're not a victim anymore. Regardless of what you've decided, making such a decision is an important milestone.

To keep things in perspective, remember that your decision to maintain a sexual secret does not have to be permanent. You can change your mind and choose to share whenever you like. You can also think of your secret as having several parts, and choose to share just one or two of them.

In this chapter we'll look at the reasons you have chosen secrecy, some possible consequences, and how you can cope with those consequences. We'll even talk a bit about when psychotherapy can be helpful.

HEALTHY AND UNHEALTHY REASONS FOR NOT SHARING

You'll recall from Chapter 8 that some reasons for sharing are much better than others. Examples of good reasons included getting closer to a partner and improving a sexual relationship. Examples of poor reasons included punishing a partner and testing a relationship. We also discussed what would indicate that sharing might be inappropriate, such as the possibility of violence or a serious lack of trust.

The Secrecy Imperative, as you know, provides most of our poor reasons for secrecy. These include the belief that our sexuality or self is bad, the fear that we will lose our relationship, and the misperception that no one else has had the sexual feelings, thoughts, and experiences we have.

Recall the reasons you have chosen to maintain your secrets. Are they healthy? (It may be helpful to review the guidelines at the beginning of Chapter 8.) How do you feel about your reasons—defeated, relaxed, confused, defensive, satisfied, frustrated?

Learning and growing leads to self-awareness, which has its painful side. With your new understanding of sexual secrets, you may be painfully aware that your reasons for secrecy are not healthy. In that case, feeling bad—foolish, angry, sad, disappointed, cheated—is appropriate. You may even get depressed.

That is exactly what happened to Jay, an older man referred to me by his minister. Jay had been going to prostitutes for several years, an activity he phased out during the four-month engagement to his second wife, Rose.

"I wanted to tell her," he said in his raspy smoker's voice, "and I still do. But I thought I was protecting her, not telling her stuff she couldn't handle. Now I realize I was afraid she would leave me. I was insecure, but for no good reason. The truth is," he said, shaking his head, "she's crazy about me.

"I feel really embarrassed," Jay continued, "like I let both of us down. I guess there's the AIDS issue to consider. Plus, now I'm nervous about the other things I haven't told her. It's all been for good reasons, or so I've thought. But now, it's hard to trust myself. Looking at this closely has thrown me into a tizzy."

You won't be surprised at my response. "Feel your feelings," I told Jay. "They're understandable. This won't be the last time you feel that way, you know.

"But don't hold on to these feelings any longer than necessary," I added. "After all, this is the first time you've ever kept a secret consciously. So mix some sympathy in with that self-criticism."

The words soothed Jay, as I hope they will soothe you. Like Jay, I'm sure you have been doing your best all along. Whether your current choice of secrecy is really good for you or not, taking deliberate action—the fact that your secrecy has been *chosen*—is an important step.

Besides, you can re-examine the issue whenever you like, whether it's a month, three months, or three years from now. You'll always have another chance to decide about your secrecy whenever you like.

Another way to benefit from making a conscious decision is by examining the way it fits in with the rest of your life. That is, the way in which we choose secrecy often reflects the way we deal with our emotions in general.

Take the time right now to examine this important source

of information about yourself. Following are three common ways a decision to maintain secrecy may mirror your larger emotional life:

1. *You see yourself weighing decisions carefully, and then backing away from assertive, healthy choices anyway.*

Stan is a married man who's starving for more affection and lovemaking. "I've read the self-help books that say I've got to be honest about what I want sexually," he says. "And from talking to people, I know that what I want is reasonable. I really can't stand the way Liz and I hardly ever have sex. But I know if I told her how much it bothers me, we'd get into a terrible fight. I don't want to deal with that right now, so I'll let it go for a while."

In addition to its impact on your sexual secrecy, passivity like this may be reflected in other ways:

- You won't stand up to your boss when you're right
- You don't always stand firm on your parenting decisions
- You say no to salesmen, and then listen to their pitch anyway; sometimes you're even intimidated into buying things you don't want

2. *You let fear cloud your thinking, which is otherwise clear.*

Unbeknownst to her husband, Martha masturbates a couple of times a week. "I know there's nothing wrong with masturbating," she says, "and Frank seems really open about sex. So I have no reason to be secretive. But I'm still afraid he'd be insulted if he found out. I would just die! I can't take that chance."

In addition to its impact on your sexual secrecy, fearfulness like this may be reflected in other ways:

- You won't volunteer for work or community assignments you know you can do
- You won't let your kids have a reasonable amount of independence

- You won't let people see your artwork, fearing that they would either dislike it or pretend to like it just to be polite

3. *You become completely absorbed by a feeling and, despite the obvious facts, tenaciously hold on to it.*

Jed was sexually abused by his mother when he was six. "I wish I could tell my finacée I was molested," he says quietly. "Everything on TV and in magazines says that the child isn't at fault, that the victim deserves sympathy, not blame. But I still feel like I somehow should have stopped it. And I feel guilty that I enjoyed my mom's attention, even though I hated what we did.

"So I just can't tell Cheryl. I honestly think it's getting in the way of my agreeing to have children. But I just can't stop thinking that I'm a pervert, you know, that I somehow seduced my mother."

Other examples of obsessing on a feeling include the following:

- You believe that your best friend's husband doesn't like you, even though he is always friendly
- You expect to somehow be punished for feeling competitive at work, and for fantasizing about ways of getting ahead
- You insist that your dad is treating you like a kid, even though he doesn't do that anymore

If you realize that you dislike your reasons for keeping secrets, you may become harshly self-critical. This punitive, unsympathetic attitude toward yourself is just another version of the self-criticism and low self-esteem that make secrecy seem crucial in the first place.

Instead of doing that to yourself, make a conscious effort to appreciate yourself this very moment. Recall some of your good intentions and honest efforts in a current or recent relationship.

Even if your reasons for not sharing are healthy ones,

there is a good chance that you will have strong feelings about your secrecy now that you're facing it honestly. To deal with these feelings, find other ways to share and be close, while still respecting the concerns that made you choose secrecy.

As one example, consider the woman who wants to explore new worlds sexually, while her partner is committed to narrow ideas about acceptable sexual expression. There are other sensual worlds this couple can explore together, such as walking in unfamiliar parks or sharing new kinds of touch, like hand or foot massage.

Such a strategy is particularly important when you have healthy motives for sharing, but also receive strong signals that sharing would be a mistake. In this type of situation, try one or more of the following:

- Read a book together (you can even read aloud to each other)
- Participate in a self-discovery workshop
- Suggest marriage counseling
- Develop a joint hobby or project
- Spend more time together as a family
- Renegotiate other parts of your relationship, such as the amount of time alone you get, or the way money is spent
- Change your own sexual behavior; for example, initiate more, or stop participating in activities you don't enjoy

THE CONSEQUENCES OF SECRECY

In Chapter 2, you became familiar with the consequences of secrecy: guilt, anxiety, anger, isolation, and sexual dissatisfaction. When you choose secrecy consciously, there is an additional consequence: the loss of innocence.

It's one thing to feel forced to be dishonest because there is something wrong with you or your sexuality. Such a distorted perspective allows you to deny many painful aspects of reality. But when we choose secrecy consciously, we admit that our relationship and our partner are not perfect. Further, we begin to relinquish the dream that our partner or relationship might be perfect in the future. Ultimately, we approach a truly profound loss: the realization that perhaps *no* relationship will ever be perfect. Maybe our dream is unrealistic.

We also suffer the loss of part of our self-image. As a conscious secret-keeper, it is difficult (or impossible) to say now, "I am always honest." Or, that "I'd never be in a relationship with someone I couldn't be open with." In a sense, we lose the self we thought we knew.

No one illustrates this better than does Grace. "I have a terrible secret, and it's killing me," she began at our very first session together."Actually, I've told several people, but not my mother. I don't see how I can. So by doing the 'right thing,' I'm hurting myself. Just what you shrinks love, huh?"

A jewelry designer, Grace had been engaged to marry a well-known computer whiz in our area. They were both young, attractive, on their way up. Everyone thought it was a match made in heaven. Then the engagement was abruptly broken. There were vague explanations, then rumors. People sensed that something wasn't right.

"Very few people knew that I had never slept with Peter," said Grace matter-of-factly. "Maybe it's weird, but I wanted sex to be special for us. We would start a new life together from scratch. Peter wasn't crazy about the idea at first, but he loved me, and he kept his sense of humor about it.

"Everything was fine until New Year's Eve," Grace continued. "We drank too much, like most people. But we were having a great time. We decided to go for a drive." I remember raising an eyebrow, unintentionally. "Yeah, I know, we shouldn't have driven after drinking. I've been all through that, okay?

"The important thing is that he raped me," Grace said bitterly. "He said I was so beautiful that he just had to touch me. I said no, he said yes, I said no, and he went crazy. Tore my dress, bruised my arm, and selfishly, brutally, took sex from me . . . his wife-to-be."

It had happened more than a year ago, and Grace had recovered about as much as any woman ever does. But she still hadn't told her mother.

"Mama was almost destroyed when I left Peter," she says. "She loved him like a son, loved him more than me, she used to joke. Some joke. It made people uncomfortable when she said that because there was a kernel of truth in it.

"Mama once told me, in fact, that she'd never forgive me if I 'lost' him or 'drove him away.' When I told her Peter and I split, she looked at me and said, 'You've finally done it, girl, you've thrown away the best thing you'll ever have.' She didn't even ask me what happened until later.

"So I've given it a lot of thought, and I've decided that it would be better for everyone if I didn't tell her. The only problem is, she thinks it's all my fault, and she's still angry at me. It's sad to lose my mama." She cried quietly.

Grace has had a terrible experience, and now she has a terrible secret. And she keeps it not because she feels inferior or inadequate, but because she has thoughtfully decided that in this less-than-perfect world, secrecy is her best course of action.

Grace is very, very hurt by the truth about the relation ship with her mother. She has been confronted by the loss of her dignity and illusions. She will never be quite the same Grace that she was before this loss, just as she will never be quite the same woman she was before the rape.

The loss of innocence affects different people in different ways. Some people feel robbed of something they are entitled to, and they get angry. They may attack the partner who seems "responsible" for this loss, even though the partner is unaware of the upheaval. Or they may turn the anger inward, manifesting it as depression.

I have heard the latter experience described in a number of ways:

- "Emotionally, I had the wind totally knocked out of me."
- "My world isn't what it used to be, and I don't especially want what's left."
- "It's totally unfair."
- "It's just my destiny to be unhappy, and there's nothing I can do."
- "I was dumb to trust or to believe. I swear I'll never do that again."
- "Nothing about life looks appealing right now."

The loss of innocence leads to these shattering, primitive feelings, says psychologist Sheldon Kopp, because "Beliefs that once served as solutions have now been transformed into problems." Childhood survival requires a belief in a fair, ordered universe. The adult realization that survival depends on keeping secrets from loved ones challenges this belief, changing it into an existential dilemma.

In therapy, I urge my clients to accept the loss of innocence, and to use it to affirm their lives. In the next section we examine the mourning process that this requires, along with other coping strategies.

RESOURCES

While conscious secrecy presents you with new challenges, it also provides you with new resources to deal with secrecy's consequences. Do you remember the distinction between privacy and secrecy discussed back in Chapter 2? If you've chosen secrecy for the right reasons, you've transformed your secrecy into privacy. That creates special resources and opportunities. Let's look at five of them:

1. *You can appreciate your decision.*

Where would you be without your ability to think, analyze, and make choices? You'd be a victim of circumstances your entire life. And if your judgment were consistently poor? In a way, you'd be even worse off. A carefully planned and executed decision is something to be proud of, particularly when it's one you could easily avoid.

Take a moment and jot down all the good reasons that you made the decision you did. In the weeks ahead, refer to this list as frequently as you need to, particularly when you are feeling guilty, sad, or lonely.

Choosing to keep secrets is difficult, but it can be a crucial way of asserting control over your life. Legendary football coach Vince Lombardi used to say, "A few people make things happen; lots of people watch things happen; and everyone else asks what happened." Now that you've chosen to be the first kind of person, celebrate!

2. *You can affirm the ways you and your partner share and relate together.*

This may seem obvious, but during the depths of disappointment and the loss of innocence, the better aspects of partnership are sometimes hard to keep in mind. Most relationships, whether with spouse, parent, child, or sibling, have recurring moments of warm connection. Recalling and valuing these can help you through your anger and loneliness.

Take Ilene, a friendly mother of two who first met me at an adult education program. She took my card at intermission, and called me a week later.

Ilene had been upset for months, it seems, and my talk had pushed her into action. "It helped me define my situation," she told me, "and sort of organize it in my mind. It also made me realize I wasn't alone."

Ilene started our session by showing me photos of her two sons. She had breast-fed the older one, and was still nursing the ten month old. Both infant and mother enjoyed it.

"But there's a problem with my husband Jim and me," she said sadly. "We still enjoy sex quite a bit, but I don't want him touching or squeezing my breasts." I nodded understandingly. "Sometimes it makes me squirt milk, which is a nuisance, but that's not really the main thing." Ilene stopped cold, turning red.

"Go on," I said gently. "You're doing fine."

"Well," she started again, "I feel so close to the baby. We've shared so much, we've been together night and day for almost a year. When he sucks, I . . . I sometimes get aroused. It's just so intimate, and it feels so good. I almost climaxed a few weeks ago."

Ilene blushed. When I told her that many women had the same experience, she relaxed a bit. "Okay, then I'll tell you the truth," she said. "Every once in a while, I do climax." She looked relieved. It was a warm moment.

"But the problem is," she resumed, "Jim doesn't know how attached I am to Geoffrey's feeding, and how much I don't want him to touch my breasts. I've wanted to tell Jim many times, but he's always teasing me about it. He even told me my time was running out, that I wasn't going to pamper Geoffrey like I did his brother.

"I've thought it all over, and it seems clear that I just shouldn't tell. But I feel terrible! What kind of way is this for the boys to start their lives? How can Jim and I ever be close again? I almost feel like I'm being unfaithful," she sniffed.

We spent most of that session talking about the dynamics of her relationships, both with her parents and her husband. When she returned the following week she was still agitated, particularly about choosing to be separate (she called it "distant") from Jim.

In addition to continuing our look at family dynamics, I wanted to help Ilene put things in perspective. For homework, I had her write down ways that she and Jim were still as connected as ever. In what ways did they still function as a happy team? How did they trust each other?

When she returned for her third session she felt much better. "I really lost track of things for a while," Ilene said. There were many ways in which she and Jim were still close: they sang in a church choir together, they spent time with another couple they both loved, they had learned Spanish together and spoke it to each other periodically—"Usually not very well, which makes us laugh a lot," Ilene noted. "And another thing—we have sex together, and it's usually pretty good."

I'll admit that I was disappointed when Ilene chose to maintain her secret from Jim. But I felt good about the ways she ultimately handled the secrecy.

Think about the many ways you and your partner share a special world together. These may include one or more of the following:

• Pet names for each other's genitals
• The Sunday morning newspaper-in-bed ritual
• Supportive and effective joint child-rearing
• Watching TV sports together
• Enjoyable sex
• Entertaining as a couple
• Supporting each other's careers
• Spending time with each other's families
• Showering together, just for fun

Feelings of distance and isolation generally occur when you keep secrets. But one of the reasons you chose secrecy is that you judged it an important way to keep the closeness you already have. Be conscious about the secrecy process, so you can enjoy that closeness.

3. *You can explore and confront the real meaning of your guilt.*

Many people who keep sexual secrets automatically feel guilty. To make sense of their guilt, they fantasize about terrible consequences and interpretations. But your secrecy does *not* necessarily mean that your relationship will die, that your sex life is doomed, that you don't care about your partner, or that you are bad.

These concerns show, once again, that when people come from a place of shame and self-doubt, their secrecy symbolizes everything they're ashamed of, which creates guilt.

But if you have chosen secrecy consciously, you need not feel guilty. You know your sexuality is not bad. You know your motives are not bad. Thus, you can know that your sexual secrecy is not bad. You do not deserve to be punished for it. There is nothing to feel guilty about.

And yet, guilt may persist. Rather than deny it or fall victim to it, *look* at it. Perhaps it's a form of anger: you resent losing some of your dreams, or being forced to realize that you're not perfect. Maybe your guilt is a way of sympathizing with your partner, who doesn't even know he or she is the object of your secrecy.

When you know that your sexuality is not bad, feeling guilty about it can be instructive. Take a moment to look at your guilt. What can you learn from it?

Keep in mind that you can be sad, embarrassed, or regretful without feeling guilty. Make sure there are people in your life supporting this healthy attitude, even if only through books or workshops. Much of our society's energy and institutions encourage you to feel guilty about your sexual thoughts and behavior, so get as much support as you need to battle this sexual tyranny.

4. *You can confide in others.*

This strategy is available primarily when you consciously *choose* secrecy. That's because you are far more likely to disclose information about yourself when you feel you are right or adequate.

Confiding in someone else can be an important source of support, emotional discharge, reality testing, and input. You may be tempted, however, to use your confidential time as an escape from your pain rather than as a productive way of coping with it. You may, for example, idealize the person in whom you are confiding.

To prevent such an occurrence, ask yourself the following:

- Does my confiding have a compulsive or addictive quality? Do I feel high before or after confiding?
- Am I confiding more than just this secret? That is, am I using this chance to get close to my confidant? Am I building up a case to justify some later action?
- How would I feel if the roles were reversed and someone were confiding this same material to me? Would I say this person was confiding in me in a healthy way, or using me to escape from his/her problems?
- Is my choice of confidant risky? How do I justify this choice to myself?
- Do I feel jealous of my confidant's other relationships? Perhaps I care more about my confidant than is appropriate.
- After I confide or discuss my secret, do I feel closer to my partner, or more distant? (This is one way to distinguish between getting support and creating an escape.)

Under some circumstances, sharing your secret with someone other than your partner can be relieving, affirming, and nurturing. Confiding is a powerful experience. As with secrecy, do it consciously, and for the right reasons.

5. *You can mourn the loss of innocence.*

The loss of innocence is a special result of conscious secret-keeping. Grief is the feeling of emptiness that follows the acknowledgment of loss. Mourning, or grieving, is the way to cope with this feeling.

Judith Viorst calls mourning "the process of adapting to the losses of our life." C. S. Lewis reminds us that, "Sorrow is not a state but a process." It also frequently signals the acceptance of change. Thus, mourning can be both painful and freeing.

Confronting the reality of our existential separateness is a good reason to mourn. We live in blissful ignorance of this separateness until about age six months. Acquiring the mental ability to distinguish between ourselves and others in infancy is the seminal moment of Paradise Lost. We spend the rest of our lives futilely attempting to deny it.

The only way to transcend this loss is to mourn and accept it, and to understand that all human beings experience this tragedy. Or, you can look at it entirely differently, as Sheldon Kopp suggests: "The only way to solve some problems is by losing serious interest in them."

So perhaps we should welcome the loss of innocence, plunging into a task which is inevitable. Resisting or denying it means giving up what little control we can have in the situation. And, of course, it neither prevents nor postpones the loss anyway.

Mourning can thus be a statement of adulthood: "I'm responsible for myself, even when I don't like the way the world is. I won't pretend to be a victim, even if it feels better." When we mourn our losses, we can better appreciate what we still have, including the power to mourn and let go of what is no longer ours.

As you mourn, reminds psychologist Melba Colgrove, don't punish yourself with "if onlys." As the saying goes, "If we had eggs, we could make ham and eggs, if only we had ham." And don't forget to forgive the person you can't share your secret with. Psychologist Kopp, ever the philosopher, notes how that person is in exactly the same boat we're in. "It's merely the ordinary state of human affairs," he says.

THERAPY, FOR BETTER OR WORSE

Marriage counseling and psychotherapy are wonderful tools. They can help you understand yourself and your partner better, and guide you to new ways of looking at things.

Just as you don't go to a dentist or car mechanic for inappropriate reasons (learning to smile better, or getting your car washed), you shouldn't go to a therapist expecting the wrong thing.

Fifty years ago, people who went to "shrinks" were considered sick or crazy. Now we know that therapy is useful for people who keep repeating the same mistakes; for people who have difficulty getting close to others; for people who have trouble getting an objective view of reality; and for people who can't be comfortable with their feelings.

These are realistic goals in therapy:

- Understanding your real reasons for choosing secrecy
- Accepting your choice of secrecy
- Understanding secrecy's real consequences
- Finding new ways of dealing with those consequences
- Getting help in preparing for future choices
- Reducing the amount of guilt you feel about your choice

But there are limits to what the tools of therapy can do within the structure of certain situations. If you want a therapist to do any of the following, you will be disappointed:

- Magically create more closeness than two partners can tolerate, particularly without changing the relationship's structure
- Improve your sex life without increasing your sharing or decreasing your anxiety
- Make secrecy a good choice, if you're doing it for bad reasons
- Approve of the secret's content if it is self-destructive
- Reduce the chances of a partner feeling angry or betrayed if he or she discovers the secret-keeping
- Give advice

Therapy provides emotional support when you're isolated, a dependable foundation from which to experiment with change, and an ally who refuses to ignore or approve of self-destructiveness.

Still, with or without therapy, each of us is ultimately alone. *The good news is,* we're not alone in this aloneness. We're all in the same empty boat.

11

BETWEEN PARENTS
AND KIDS

Never have children, only grandchildren.
—GORE VIDAL

Human beings are sexual from the womb to the tomb.
—MARY CALDERONE

In chapters 1 through 10 we discussed issues arising from the fact that children keep sexual secrets from their parents. This chapter is about the sexual secrets that parents keep from their kids.

"But," many parents say, "That's not secrecy—that's natural. Besides," they argue,

- "I'm just too embarrassed to talk about it."
- "My silence is for my child's own good."
- "I don't know what to say to her."
- "I'm just being neutral. I don't want to encourage her."
- "He doesn't need that kind of information yet."

Recall our definition of sexual secrecy: Relevant information about sexuality withheld from important others. This is "natural" only in the sense that parents' discomfort about their children's sexuality is very common. It is this discomfort that generally leads to parents keeping sexual secrets from their children.

Common subjects of this sexual secrecy include:

- Masturbation
- Contraception
- The innate wholesomeness of sexuality
- The fact that sex feels good
- The sexuality of parents, especially single parents
- The importance of talking seriously about sex
- Healthy ways to make sexual decisions
- Information about the body
- The reality that children, too, have sexual feelings

REASONS FOR KEEPING SEXUAL SECRETS FROM CHILDREN

By now, you know that we keep sexual secrets for reasons of which we're not entirely aware. Keeping secrets is a way of acting out certain fears—about ourselves, our relationships, and our sexuality. It's the same with our children. Keeping sexual secrets from them is a way of acting out our fears and anxieties.

Let's look at the various dynamics behind this secrecy.

Denial of sexual reality

In Chapter 5, denial was described as a way of avoiding painful feelings. Some parents find the fact that their children are sexual just too hard to handle. As part of denying this reality, they believe that their kids have no need for sexual information.

I'm reminded of a woman named Trudy who came to me because her ten-year-old son Josh was, as she put it, "obsessed with sex." Apparently, he was a very curious boy, "always asking questions, wanting to look at sexy magazines, looking at his sister's biology books . . . he's even peeked at her in the shower a few times lately," she told me.

While Trudy was deeply disturbed by Josh's "obsession," I wondered if it wasn't just normal childhood sexual curiosity. Nothing she said suggested that the boy had any serious problems. The main point she kept repeating in various ways was that he was interested in sex, which seemed to frighten and confuse her greatly.

I knew that Trudy was a single mother with sexual issues of her own. "I don't need it anymore," she told me flatly. "It was miserable when I was married, and now I'm done with it." Didn't she miss the companionship of a lover, male or female? "No," she insisted. "Josh and I are great pals. That's enough for me." I began to suspect that unconsciously, Trudy didn't want Josh to grow up and leave her.

I asked Trudy how she could tell the difference between a child's healthy interest in sex and an unhealthy interest. Although I asked twice, she seemed not to understand the question. I asked her if perhaps Josh was simply trying to learn about sex any way he could. After all, his father wasn't around and his mother wasn't all that open about it.

"He *can't* need that kind of information," Trudy said, bewildered and a bit angry. "He's only ten years old." Unlike his curiosity about engines or forestry, Josh's interest in sex had no legitimacy to his mother. "He just can't be interested in that," she said. "He's so pure. He's practically a baby."

Gradually, we were getting to the truth. Trudy had been raised to believe that sex was dirty. The sex in her marriage had been clumsy and painful, reinforcing that belief. Trudy could not believe that her precious son could be involved in something dirty and destructive like sexuality. She avoided the painful reality by denying it.

Instead of agreeing that Josh was the problem, I worked with Trudy on her own sexual feelings. She became aware of her fear and anger about sex, and of how these had affected her marriage. She also became increasingly aware of how these feelings were affecting her now.

Eventually, Trudy was able to agree that Josh should have a healthy sex life in his future marriage—"not like I had," she said ruefully. Using mental imagery, we visited the future and observed Josh's marriage, including his healthy sexual relationship. "I'm jealous," Trudy laughed at one point. From there, we worked backward, visualizing the kind of adolescence and childhood Josh would need to create that satisfying adulthood. This would have to include the recognition of his healthy sexual interest *in the present.*

"It hurts, but I have to do it," said Trudy, beginning to cry. "Whether I pretend or not, he's going to grow up, isn't he?" Predictably, working through her own sexuality enabled Trudy to deal with her son's. She didn't even need much coaching about what to say.

As I sat with Trudy, I recalled the words of pioneer sex educator Dr. Mary Calderone: "You're not just sex educating your child about sexuality, you're also sex educating someone's future spouse, someone's future parent."

Some parents feel terribly threatened by the healthy separation that they and their children must eventually experience. The challenge of this painful separation is underscored by the child's connections with others. Since sexuality symbolizes the transfer of a child's intimacy from parent to peer, denying that sexuality can be a way for parents to avoid that painful loss.

These families would be far better off if the adults learned to confront their own sexual and emotional feelings. Many parents have still not accepted their *own* sexuality, which makes accepting their *kids'* sexuality even more painful. Again, secrecy can be a way for parents to avoid facing painful sexual realities.

Embarrassment

"Speak the truth and shame the Devil," said the French humanist Rabelais in 1552. Lacking his courage—or disdain for decorum—most of us often silence ourselves through sexual secrecy when we are simply too embarrassed to speak the truth.

Parents are embarrassed about sex for a variety of reasons. You may have been taught that sex is not fit for serious or gentle conversation. You may have no comfortable language with which to discuss sex. There's a big, awkward gap between "poo-poo" and "labia majora." Most of us would blush to hear our children say "cock," and saying it ourselves isn't much easier.

Much embarrassment comes from feeling inadequate. "I can't stand telling my kid that I don't know some basic thing about fallopian tubes," one mother told me, "when I've been having sex for twenty years."

We don't presume to know everything about stoves simply because we cook. Why, then, do we expect ourselves to be technically sophisticated about sexuality?

Feeling awkward about your own sexuality certainly makes it more difficult to deal with your child's. "He asks me if his penis is big enough," a father once wrote to me. "I'm still not confident that *mine* is! So what am I supposed to tell him?"

Ways to deal with embarrassment are covered in some detail below. For now, rest assured that embarrassment is normal, and that you can always answer questions by starting with, "Well, this is embarrassing for me, Jimmy, but here goes . . ."

Fear of harming children

In general, ours is a culture that believes in knowledge. Americans value their schools, libraries, and degrees. We push our children to learn as much as they can, as fast as they can.

What a contrast to cultures that believe knowledge is

dangerous, such as Europe during the Dark Ages. We Americans pride ourselves on our nonsuperstitious approach to knowledge. We know, for example, that driver education doesn't cause car accidents.

While this sounds simple, it is a concept that many parents find hard to apply to sexuality. But the data has been clear for years: *Reliable sexual information does not create destructive teenage sexual behavior.*

According to a well-known study in 1977, for example, sociologists Zelnik and Kantner found that American kids from families in which sexuality is discussed openly make healthier sexual decisions. They tend to postpone intercourse, compared with their peers, and are more likely to use contraception the first time they have intercourse. This finding was replicated in 1987, by the way, in a study of the Baltimore school system.

Similarly, in Swedish families, where sex is discussed more freely than in comparable American families, roughly 90 percent of the teenagers use contraception the first time they have intercourse. In this country the figure is roughly 10 percent. And it's not because Swedish kids are inherently smarter than American kids.

Most adolescent sexual problems are caused by poor decision-making. The alternative is better sexual decision-making—which requires information, guidance, and values. Ignoring sexuality, or simply saying "Don't do it," provides none of these. A prohibitive, deliberately neglectful approach maintains sexual ignorance, which leads to poor decisions.

Some parents are afraid that they will say the wrong thing, or say too much, and thereby damage a child who can't handle it. But you already know how children react when you try to tell them something beyond their interest or understanding. They get bored and distracted, and try to get away as soon as possible. This is exactly how kids handle sexual material that's over their heads. It doesn't damage them; they just tune it out.

This brings to mind the story of the five-year-old who asked the proverbial "Where do I come from?" question one day. Her modern father had read the books, and knew this was a moment to be savored and used, not squandered. Wanting to do it right, he gave her an elaborate explanation of reproductive physiology. "Now," he asked with a smile when finished, "do you have any questions?" "Just one," said the child intently. "Janet says she's from Philadelphia. Where do I come from?"

If you think of sex as dangerous, it is natural to want to protect your children from it. What's dangerous, however, is poor sexual decision-making, stemming from a *lack* of knowledge.

By all means, protect your kids from *this*—through education. Make certain they get quality information and your caring attention so that they can make intelligent sexual decisions. This means, of course, acknowledging that sexual feelings, issues, and decisions exist in your child's life.

Pain and adversity in childhood

Parents must recognize that children cannot be protected from every possible experience of pain. While all parents wish they could, it's simply impossible. Experts agree that protecting children in this way isn't even desirable. Children need to learn that they can adequately cope with pain and adversity so that it does not debilitate them when it comes their way in adulthood.

And yet, certain unrealistic parents persist in trying to help their children avoid any pain associated with sexuality. In doing so they teach the lesson that sex is dangerous, and that the child cannot trust him/herself to deal with it. This, ironically, is the very background that leads to sexual problems (such as date rape and inhibited sexual desire) in later life.

The commitment to *prevent* any pain in a child's life, then, is actually destructive. If, for instance, you are determined that your babies will never fall down, you will prevent them from ever learning to walk. They will be functionally crippled. This is a form of child abuse. So is the childrearing that produces adults who are sexually crippled.

RESULTS OF SECRECY

As a result of secrecy, kids develop incorrect and even damaging ideas about sexuality and themselves. They learn that sex is somehow bad, although they are never told why. They learn to feel bad about having sexual feelings, although again, they don't know why.

Using the normal simplistic reasoning of childhood, young people conclude they are somehow defective. They learn to feel guilty just for being who they are.

Some of the wrong ideas that uninformed kids get are funny—for example, that twins are caused by hiccups during pregnancy. Some ideas are not so funny, such as that sex is the way you prove you love someone. And some myths are downright dangerous, such as the common idea that you can't get pregnant if you have sex standing up.

Secrecy prevents children from learning the concept of good sexual decision-making. Parents teach kids good decision-making in other areas: how to identify and select healthy foods, for example, or how to choose warm, nurturing friends.

But instead of teaching kids how to make good sexual decisions, we either say "Don't do it," or we refuse to mention sex at all. Neither is helpful when young people get into confusing or dangerous sexual situations.

We also teach young people not to talk to us about their sexual concerns. We label sexual interest "bad," pretend that *our* children have none, and threaten to punish them if they do. So naturally, when they have some sex-related problem, they hide it from their parents. Eventually, the parent finds out, and demands, "Why didn't you come to me?" The answer is simple: all their lives, young people have been instructed not to.

Finally, parental sexual secrecy heightens children's vulnerability to sexual exploitation. Kids' lack of pride in, or sense of ownership of their bodies, and their sense of shame and guilt about sex, reduces their power to prevent it.

Unless they learn about the wholesomeness of their bodies and sexuality, kids have trouble saying no to adults who want to molest them. As teens, they are vulnerable to peers who demand they prove their love through sex. And as adults, they may lack the self-esteem to resist the pressure that sometimes results in acquaintance rape.

Ultimately, because all normal kids have sexual feelings and questions, your refusal to acknowledge or answer them can make you the enemy. This adversarial situation is the saddest consequence of all.

Here are some common sexual messages that young people get from their parents' sexual secrecy:

- Sex is dangerous
- Sex can hurt you
- Sex is only for bad girls
- Sex is a big problem between men and women
- Your body is bad
- It's bad to feel good
- You shouldn't be in charge of your own body
- Planning or communicating about sex is bad
- Good people don't get exploited sexually
- If you are sexually victimized it's your fault
- Males are only interested in sex
- Females aren't really interested in sex
- If you have sexual feelings, it must be love
- Don't trust your feelings

PARENTAL RESPONSIBILITY

Family sex education never really stops.

Just as your children observe your table manners every

time you eat with them, they also observe your messages about sexuality. They're sensitive to their environment, picking up cues that reveal your true feelings and beliefs.

The situation personifies what Emerson meant when he said, "Who you are speaks so loudly, I cannot hear what you say."

So sex education isn't an event, it's a continuing process. It isn't a conversation that you do or don't have with kids. It's a pervasive attitude in the home—between parents, between parent and child, and within the child and his or her self.

Here are some examples of typical sex education scenes that children absorb in different kinds of homes:

Positive:
- Parents habitually touch each other affectionately "for no reason"; touching does not automatically lead to sex
- A child occasionally sees her father in his underwear without a fuss being made
- One parent good-naturedly teases the other about being interested in sex

Negative:
- A parent punishes the family dog for licking its genitals
- When Father drinks he always tries to sloppily kiss Mom, who always pushes him away
- Parents make constant reference to certain neighborhood women as "sluts"

While the specifics of such subtle lessons are easily forgotten over time, they shape a child's vision of sexuality and relationships for life. Remember, parents are the primary sexuality educators of their children, whether they like it or not.

Most parents are glad to have this much influence over their child's developing values and personality. At the same time, however, it is a reminder that your home and sexual attitudes aren't solely your own affair. Their effect on your children must be considered.

This is a familiar idea in other contexts. You may prefer glass table lamps, say, but if you have toddlers, you buy furnishings of plastic or other unbreakable materials to accommodate the needs of your little ones.

"Don't I have the right," parents sometimes ask, "to decide for myself whether or not to discuss sex with my child?" The answer is a resounding *no*. You can choose *what* to share with them, but their emotional health demands that you somehow acknowledge the reality of sexuality in their lives. As with many other parental responsibilities, you may not *like* it, but you do it because it's part of being a parent.

Parenthood demands that you give your children information about basic subjects like health, money, food, and religion. Sexuality is no different. Ignoring, minimizing, or rejecting the parental obligation of sexuality education is irresponsible.

AIDS AND PARENTS

One example of parental responsibility is educating children about AIDS. According to the Surgeon General of the United States, you should start doing this by the time a child is eight, supplementing whatever program the school offers.

To do so, most parents unselfishly need to set aside their own discomfort. Some, however, refuse. Instead, they act out their own feelings, fulfilling their own needs at the expense of their children's welfare.

A man whom I'll call Alexander is a good example. A parent and member of a school board two counties over from mine, he had fought every AIDS education program the junior high school had tried to set up, including a session to train teachers.

When asked to explain his position, he usually replied that kids had no need for the information. "The people pushing these programs are sick," he said in an interview. "They're putting sexual ideas into innocent kids' heads."

At the height of his involvement in the school controversy, Alexander was in a debate that ended in a rowdy, physical free-for-all. Four people were hurt, and seven arrested—including Alexander. As part of his probation he was sent to therapy, and agreed to see me.

"Seeing an out-of-town counselor will make it a little more private," he said when we met. I generally don't accept court-ordered cases, but I was interested in the chance to work with a radically anti-sex public figure.

Over the course of six sessions Alexander and I discussed philosophy, politics, science, and as much about him as he would allow. One day we talked about his college experiences, and he revealed that both his freshman- and sophomore-year roommates were gay.

Apparently it was a coincidence. They didn't even know each other. "But they were like two peas in a pod," Alexander said bitterly. "They didn't have the decency to tell me the very first day. No, they were friendly, like regular guys. I spent time with them, got to like them real well. *Then* they lowered the boom.

"It troubled me, scared me," Alexander said with more emotion than he'd expressed in our other sessions. "How come I didn't know? How could I actually like these queers, these perverts? When I found out, I kicked them out. Two in a row—1966, 1967. What else could I do?"

Alexander was done with his story. I wasn't. "What happened then?" I asked. "Did you miss them?"

"That was the worst," Alexander said, his voice suddenly soft. "I did miss them. Jack had been my best pal. Scott was my bridge partner. He'd show me his short stories, I'd show him my poems. Yes, I missed them," said Alexander. "I thought about them, cursed them. Eventually, I got over it, though." His voice started getting its edge back.

I felt sad for Alexander's loss. "And have you missed

either one since?" I asked. He had. "It was about a year after my wife and I moved here from Chicago," he said, "about three years ago. I was lonely. I dreamed about them about a half-dozen times. In one I asked them to take me with them. I woke up feeling ashamed and disgusted."

"Wasn't that about when you became involved in the anti-AIDS education thing?" I asked. He eyed me suspiciously, nodded yes, and suddenly became teary. He was using the AIDS issue to act out his own fears about homosexuality. He was hurting his kids—and everyone else's—but he couldn't help it. He couldn't even see it. Unfortunately, that didn't make him any less destructive.

I'd like to tell you that this one has a happy ending, but it doesn't. Alexander was not really interested in understanding himself better, nor in being more responsible to his family and community. "You don't understand," he told me when he had completed his required number of sessions. "None of you queer-lovers do."

There is nothing wrong with having strong feelings about sex educating your child. As with other feelings, you must simply find a way to deal with them that does not compromise the health and safety of your children and spouse. There is almost always a more productive alternative than keeping dangerous sexual secrets from them.

DEALING WITH YOUR FEELINGS

How, then, shall you handle your feelings about being involved in your child's sex education? With the same approach we have discussed throughout this book: acknowledge them, accept them, and get support for them.

First you must recognize what those feelings are. At the beginning of this chapter we discussed the difficulties most parents have accepting the sexuality of their children. Issues about separation are often triggered when we were confronted with our own sexual anxieties and the pain of getting older. And, of course, we worry that our kids will somehow get hurt.

The important thing is to allow yourself to have such feelings, and not to deny or discount them. Ways to accept your feelings include:

- Admit out loud that *you* have needs, and that they are okay
- See the larger context of your pain within the overall responsibilities of parenting (you already do that in other areas, such as letting your child play high school sports)
- Share *some* of your concerns with your child, such as, "This is hard for me, Troy"
- Sit quietly and imagine what your child needs from you in this special area. How does this compare with what you needed as a kid that age?
- Speak to your spouse or close friend about your concerns
- Join a group of other parents to share victories, defeats, and ideas
- Seek professional help—your choices include psychologists, marriage and family therapists, clergy, physicians, social workers, and counselors at your child's school

Perhaps most important of all, keep your sense of humor. An eye like Bill Cosby's sees the bittersweet human condition all around us: "My eleven-year-old daughter mopes around the house all day waiting for her breasts to grow."

THE ASKABLE PARENT

The opposite of being a secretive parent is being an askable parent. How do you become one?

- By knowing your sexual values
- By portraying those values honestly, without apology
- By acknowledging that sexuality exists, and that your children have sexual feelings and concerns

- By making it clear that all questions about sex are okay
- By admitting you don't know everything about sex
- By offering to help your children learn about the facts and their personal sexual concerns

If you generally present this attitude, you will develop great credibility with your children. They will understand that you want to nurture, not squelch, their healthy sexuality. And they will be more open to your ideas about making good sexual decisions.

Children with askable parents are more likely to ask— and to listen. They are more open to being guided. Denial and secrecy do not accomplish this.

The values inherent in being an askable parent also make things clearer for you. How do you handle your youngster's masturbating in the supermarket, for example? Affirm his or her sexuality, while placing it in your value context: "Yes, that feels good, but we save touching our private places for when we're at home, in private."

Children with askable parents are less apt to use sex as a weapon against their parents, because they haven't learned that sex is a bad thing. And they don't use it against themselves, because they haven't learned that they are bad, deserving punishment for sexual thoughts.

Let's look at how an askable parent might handle a few common sexual concerns.

HANDLING SOME COMMON QUESTIONS

Although every child is unique, most children present their parents with a well-known set of sexual concerns. Although all of those questions can't be listed here, a few are asked and answered below. They follow the ideal of being an askable parent, of positively shaping your child's image of sexuality and him- or herself.

The following answers are not intended to close their

respective conversations. On the contrary; they are just the beginning. Your smile and gentle tone should encourage more questions and discussion on each of these topics.

Q: Jason's mother told us that touching yourself "down there" is wrong and that God would hate me if I did it. That's not what you told me. Who is right?

A: Sometimes there is no answer that's right for every family. In your Uncle Herb's house, for instance, everybody must eat every single thing on their dinner plate. You know that we don't have that rule here.

Beliefs about touching yourself are like that too. Your father and I feel that your body is one of God's wonderful creations, and that the good feelings you get from touching it are God's gift. As long as you do it in private, we're sure it's perfectly all right.

In Great-Grandma's time lots of people felt like Jason's mother does now. I guess some people's ideas change faster than others'.

Q: What are rubbers?

A: Like most adults, your mom and I have sex because we enjoy it. When we don't want to make a baby during sex, we have to use a method of birth control. Rubbers—or condoms, prophylactics—are one such method. A rubber fits over the penis when the man puts it into a woman's vagina. It keeps his sperm from getting to her egg, which is the way babies start.

Q: What is a homosexual?

A: A homosexual is a person who has romantic, sexual feelings for someone of the same sex. No one knows why some people have these feelings for their own sex, while others have them for the other sex, but I agree with the doctors and scientists who say that homosexuals—or gays—are basically normal people.

Although there are millions and millions of homosexuals in the U.S., you can't tell who they are just by looking at or listening to them. Unfortunately, some people think that homosexuals are evil or sick, and they treat them cruelly. This is as bad as mistreating people just because they are, say, black or Jewish.

For many more sample questions, with extraordinarily wise and warm answers, see *Talking with Your Child About Sex* by Mary Calderone and James Ramey and *Raising a Child Conservatively in a Sexually Permissive World* by Sol and Judith Gordon.

"There are *limits, right?"*

"When you're eight years old, nothing is any of your business," satirist Lenny Bruce once said.

The truth, of course, is that a certain amount of what you think, feel, and do *is* none of your kids' business, regardless of their age. In the realm of sexuality, those things can include:

- What positions you use for intercourse
- How often you make love
- How many sexual partners you had before marrying
- What your spouse looks like naked
- How your partner acts during lovemaking or orgasm
- What your genitals look like

Yes, children do ask about such things. Setting limits here is more than appropriate, it is crucial. Not only does it give you the sexual privacy you need, it models the belief that everyone deserves that privacy.

A common question that arises in this area concerns children walking in on you during lovemaking. Don't hesitate to honor your need for privacy—quickly reassure your child that things are fine, and tell him or her to get out—

now! As Sol Gordon says, "Next morning you can say 'please.' "

In deciding what you will withhold and what you will share, you have to balance your need for privacy with your kids' need for sexuality education. Ideally, your choices should be based on a positive sense of what feels right to you, rather than on a negative sense of guilt or shame about sexuality.

Make sure your children understand this when you refuse their request for information you deem too personal (such a refusal, by the way, is one way of teaching modesty). Of course, if your refusal is based on the belief that sex is bad, your kids will sense that. They'll know you're keeping a sexual secret from them. Inevitably, they'll wonder what's wrong with *them*.

A child's inappropriate request is also an opportunity to demonstrate that in a close relationship, people can say no to each other without being angry. Saying no should not hurt the relationship with your child in any way.

Certainly, he or she doesn't need to feel rejected. Rather, the child can appreciate your willingness to set limits that feel good to you. These limits mean you can be trusted: they suggest that when you do answer a personal question, you feel okay about it. Remind your children that this shows they can ask you whatever they want.

SEXUAL EXPLOITATION: SECRET NO LONGER

What's worse than being sexually victimized? Being victimized and feeling guilty about it, and therefore feeling obliged to hide it. Surely, no clear-thinking parent wants his or her child to conceal such information.

And yet, we encourage this response by our attitudes about sexuality. We teach kids not to talk about sex; that being sexual is wrong; that "good" people do not sexually assault or get assaulted; and that a certain amount of violence is inherent in sexuality. And so when young people are victimized (which occurs in about one out of ten families), they know they must keep it a secret from you. In effect, they are doubly victimized.

Some parents believe that sexual secrecy prevents victimization. On the contrary—it actually makes it *more* likely. When we break that secrecy by teaching kids to like and own their bodies, and that their feelings count, they learn to say no and to prevent sexual molestation. We must tell kids that *"If you are molested, it is not your fault, and I won't be mad at you."*

SEX AND THE SINGLE PARENT

In addition to the sexual issues facing all parents, single parenthood presents special difficulties with regard to family sexuality education and sexual secrecy.

In single-parent families, the issues of connection and separation are usually still painful. Death or divorce have presented both child and parent with irreplaceable losses.

There is also a dissonance between society's idealizations about what family life should be like, and the way it really is in these families. In particular, resources that support intimacy, such as time, attention, energy, and privacy, are often badly lacking.

Most single parents would like their children eventually to have fulfilling sexual relationships. Yet, modeling such a relationship is a difficult task. Obstacles include the parent's guilt and anxiety, as well as the child's jealousy and anger.

"Trickiest of all," says one single mother, "is giving kids the message that it's better to have sex within a strong, loving relationship. How can I guide them toward this value when some of my own sexual exploits are casual? Or even when they are serious, but *look* casual to the kids?"

Good question. There is no perfect answer because society still has not come to grips with the sexual and social needs of single adults. Religious and government leaders suggest that such adults remain celibate, which is unrealistic and mean-spirited. It certainly doesn't teach children anything positive about sex.

The best solution is presenting your children with the truth as you experience it. That is, seize the initiative, and portray the meaning of your choices as *you* understand and value them, rather than letting other people or institutions define them for you.

The messages single parents probably wish to give their children include:

- A single person has friends of both genders
- A single person needs affection and intimacy, and considers this need healthy
- There is an important difference between sex and affection
- Clear sexual decision-making is important: since things are not always as they seem, we must think before we act
- A single person needs privacy
- Some things are none of the child's business

Remember: Your attitude about sexuality and intimacy, and your openness to your child's sexual concerns, are the most important sex education your children get.

"The biggest sexual secret *I'm* trying to keep from my kids," says one friend, "is that I'm not entirely on top of this sex thing."

This is probably the most common sexual secret that parents keep. Ironically, your children probably sense that on some level. After all, they know you're imperfect about everything else, right?

Accordingly, the most important thing you can teach your children about sex is that *it's okay* not to know everything about it. The appropriate response is to laugh about your embarrassment, research your ignorance, and understand that sex is not a deadly, grim subject.

This perspective puts people in charge of their sexuality, rather than at the mercy of it. There is no bigger gift a parent can give a child.

LOOKING AHEAD

Look ahead to your future sexuality and relationships. You've earned the privilege, and you're better equipped to do it now than you were the first time you opened this book.

This is what I hope you see:

• You own your sexuality, and accept your sexual thoughts, feelings, and preferences. You understand that this self-acceptance is the cornerstone of your sexual and emotional relationships.

• You may choose to share information that you've been keeping secret; you may not. If you don't, it's because you *choose* not to, not because you feel guilty, abnormal, or forced to.

• You understand that sexual secrecy often helps create and maintain the personal and relationship problems it is supposed to solve.

• If you are a parent, you recognize your active responsibility to educate your children about sexuality.

• You know that you are bigger than your sexuality. You know that your sexuality isn't dangerous, doesn't control you, and is only part of who you are.

• You have taken a step out of the harsh wilderness of self-criticism and denial toward the lush valley of self-acceptance. The emotional storms of feeling judged and abnormal are subsiding.

As Solomon sang,

Arise, my love!

For now the winter is past, the rains are over and gone.

Flowers blossom on the earth; the time of the singing of birds
is come, and the voice of the turtledove is heard in our
land.

Arise, my darling; come away!

BIBLIOGRAPHY

ATWATER, LYNN. *The Extramarital Connection*. New York: Irvington, 1982.

BARBACH, LONNIE. *Pleasures*. New York: Harper & Row, 1984.

BARDWICK, JUDITH. *In Transition*. New York: Holt, Rinehart, & Winston, 1979.

BERNE, ERIC. *Games People Play*. New York: Grove, 1964.

BLUM, GLORIA and BARRY BLUM. *Feeling Good About Yourself*. Mill Valley, California: Feeling Good Associates. 1981.

CALDERONE, MARY and JAMES RAMEY. *Talking with Your Child About Sex*. New York: Random House, 1982.

CASSELL, CAROL. *Swept Away*. New York: Bantam, 1985.

COLGROVE, MELBA et al. *How to Survive the Loss of a Love*. New York: Bantam, 1976.

FRIDAY, NANCY. *My Secret Garden*. New York: Pocket Books, 1983.

GOLDMAN, RONALD & JULIETTE. *Children's Sexual Thinking*. London: Routledge & Kegan Paul, 1982.

GORDON, SOL. *The New You*. Fayetteville, New York: Ed-U-Press, 1980.

GORDON, SOL and JUDITH GORDON. *Raising A Child Conservatively in a Sexually Permissive World*. New York: Fireside/Simon & Schuster, 1983.

HITE, SHERE. *The Hite Report on Male Sexuality*. New York: Knopf, 1981.

KOPP, SHELDON. *An End to Innocence*. New York: Bantam, 1978.

LEVINE, LINDA and LONNIE BARBACH. *The Intimate Male*. Garden City, New York: Anchor Press/Doubleday, 1983.

MILLER, ALICE. *The Drama of the Gifted Child*. New York: Basic Books, 1981.

MILLS, C. WRIGHT. *Power, Politics, and People*. London: Oxford University Press, 1967.

The New Catholic Encyclopedia. Nashville, TN: T. Nelson, 1976 (vol. 14).

NIN, ANAIS. *In Favor of the Sensitive Man and other essays*. New York: Harvest/Harcourt Brace Jovanovich, 1976.

TENNOV, DOROTHY. *Love and Limerance*. New York: Stein & Day, 1986.

VIORST, JUDITH. *Necessary Losses*. New York: Simon & Schuster, 1986.

ZELNIK and KANTNER. "Sexual and Contraceptive Experience of Young Unmarried Women in the U.S.," *Family Planning Perspectives,* 1977, IX(2), pp. 55–71.

ZILBERGELD, BERNIE. *Male Sexuality*. Boston: Little, Brown, 1978.

ZILBERGELD, BERNIE and ARNOLD LAZARUS. *Mind Power*. Boston: Little, Brown, 1987.

For further reading:

ADAMS, JANE. *Sex and the Single Parent.* New York: Coward, McCann, & Geoghegan, 1978.

BARBACH, LONNIE. *For Yourself.* New York: Doubleday, 1975.

CARRERA, MICHAEL. *Sex: The Facts, The Acts, and Your Feelings.* New York: Crown, 1981.

CLARK, DON. *The New Loving Someone Gay.* Berkeley, California: Celestial Arts, 1987.

DINNERSTEIN, DOROTHY. *The Mermaid & the Minotaur.* New York: Harper & Row, 1976.

DODSON, BETTY. *Sex for One.* New York: Crown, 1987.

EHRENREICH, BARBARA. *The Hearts of Men.* Garden City, New York: Anchor Press/Doubleday, 1984.

FREUD, SIGMUND. *Three Essays on the Theory of Sexuality.* New York: Hogarth, 1965.

GORDON, SOL. *When Living Hurts.* New York: Dell, 1988.

HITE, SHERE. *The Hite Report on Female Sexuality.* New York: Dell, 1976.

NORWOOD, ROBIN. *Women Who Love Too Much.* Los Angeles: Jeremy Tarcher, 1985.

OFFIT, AVODAH. *Night Thoughts.* New York: Congdon & Lattes, 1981.

SATIR, VIRGINIA. *Peoplemaking.* Palo Alto, California: Science & Behavior Books, 1972.

STEINER, CLAUDE. *Scripts People Live.* New York: Bantam, 1974.